Praise for

WALDEN FOR HIRE

Just when you think you know the nineteenth-century writer, environmentalist, and activist Henry David Thoreau, it turns out you don't know him at all. Ken Lizotte's *Walden for Hire* shines new light on the business savvy and accomplishments of the famed *Walden* author. Through original research and expert interviews, Lizotte describes, among other examples, how Thoreau revolutionized American pencil manufacturing and transformed a nascent surveying business through novel marketing innovations—all in the mid-1800s. But wait—there is more! Lizotte also translates these experiences into compelling business lessons that resonate with entrepreneurs today. *Walden for Hire* reminds us that a curious, persistent manner and a rewarding work life can lead us to less work and more time to actually enjoy life!

—DEBORAH LEE JAMES,
twenty-third secretary of the US Air Force and author of
Aim High: Chart Your Course and Find Success (Post Hill Press)

While there has been much already written about American naturalist and philosopher Henry David Thoreau, one might wonder what else can or needs to be said. However, in his engaging, entertaining, and eye-opening new book, *Walden for Hire*, Concord-based author and thoughtleader Ken Lizotte—who himself marches to the beat of a "different drummer"—introduces us to the business side of Thoreau, to help us see the man and his work through a fresh new lens—that of businessman and solopreneur. Filled from start to finish with fascinating facts, figures, and anecdotes from Thoreau's era, Lizotte, a master storyteller, leads us on a wonderful journey back to the past to teach us a thing or two about the business world of the present . . . while inspiring us to envision how we each might apply these insights in the future. After all, as Thoreau himself famously wrote, "The question is not what you look at, but what you see."

TODD CHERCHES,
CEO of BigBlueGumball, and author of
*VisuaLeadership: Leveraging the Power of Visual
Thinking in Leadership and in Life* (Post Hill Press)

Think you know all there is to know about Henry David Thoreau? Think again . . . better yet, read Ken Lizotte's sauntering, stereotype-busting *Walden for Hire*. Turns out that in addition to writing poetry, building his pondside cabin, and avoiding mundane jobs, Henry was by nature a savvy businessman—a surveyor without peer and a pencil-making magnate, not to mention an example for Sylvester Stallone's *Rocky*. Who knew?

—ROB MITCHELL,
founder of Concord Festival of Authors and
author of *Bat Attitude: The Soul of a Senior Softball Team*

I was actually in the woods when I received my initial peek at Ken Lizotte's *Walden for Hire*, and I was there precisely because my early experience with Henry David Thoreau created a foundation for how I would engage in the natural world my whole life. Imagine my delight to have such an inspired, closer conversation with Thoreau through Lizotte's book about how to live my working life more deliberately! The provocative wisdom of Thoreau—at his core the ultimate entrepreneur!—is exactly what I needed to read right now. Quick! Grab your No. 2 pencil and scribble your own notes in the margins!

Lizotte is the perfect person to bring *Walden for Hire* to both business entrepreneurs and Thoreau fans—he's devoted his own life to supporting the good work of thoughtleaders, speakers, and writers, living just a few miles away from Walden Pond and supporting this Concord legacy through two collections of essays. As a poet, writer, and entrepreneur, I didn't know I needed to read this book right now—to remember and reframe Thoreau's wisdom beyond the scope of that little lake in Massachusetts and to refresh my approach to my work.

—LIBBY WAGNER,
poet, speaker and business consultant,
and author of *The Influencing Option: The Art
of Building a Profit Culture in Business* (Stylus)

Through *Walden for Hire*, Ken Lizotte (a true Thoreau expert living in Concord, Massachusetts!) introduces the reader to a new appreciation of Henry David Thoreau and his wisdom. Lizotte takes one of America's most celebrated thinkers and reframes him in an entirely new light as an entrepreneur, innovator, and practical business mind. With wit, insight, and practical lessons, Lizotte explores this overlooked side of Thoreau, showing how his disciplined creativity, ethical compass, and entrepreneurial daring still offer lessons for today's leaders. I was particularly drawn to the chapter on Thoreau's "dark side," which I had never encountered before, and the way Thoreau used his writing to manage his depression. This book doesn't just reintroduce Thoreau; it reintroduces the very idea of what it means to live and work with purpose. *Walden for Hire* is a must-read for anyone who believes that business ultimately should be as much about meaning as it is about money.

—J. D. PINCUS,
PhD, author of *The Emotionally Agile Brain: Mastering the 12 Emotional Needs That Drive Us* (Bloomsbury)

WALDEN FOR HIRE

WALDEN FOR HIRE

Business Lessons from Henry David Thoreau

KEN LIZOTTE

HarperCollins
Leadership

An Imprint of HarperCollins

Walden for Hire
© 2026 by Ken Lizotte

Published by HarperCollins Leadership, an imprint of HarperCollins Focus LLC,
501 Nelson Place, Nashville, TN 37214, USA.

Any internet addresses, phone numbers, or company or product information
printed in this book are offered as a resource and are not intended in any way to be
or to imply an endorsement by HarperCollins Leadership, nor does HarperCollins
Leadership vouch for the existence, content, or services of these sites, phone
numbers, companies, or products beyond the life of this book.

"PBS" and the "PBS logo" are registered trademarks of the Public
Broadcasting Service and are used with permission. All rights reserved.

ISBN 978-1-4002-5384-5 (ePub)
ISBN 978-1-4002-5383-8 (TP)

HarperCollins Publishers, Macken House, 39/40 Mayor Street Upper, Dublin 1,
D01 C9W8, Ireland (https://www.harpercollins.com)

Library of Congress Control Number: 2025947498

Art direction: Ron Huizinga
Cover design: Faceout Studio
Interior Design: Neuwirth & Associates, Inc.

Printed in the United States of America
25 26 27 28 29 LBC 5 4 3 2 1

CONTENTS

This book is dedicated to my colleagues on the current Thoreau Farm Trust Board of Directors, especially Molly Q. Eberle, Nancy McJennett, Court Booth, and the late, great Joe Wheeler. For over twenty years, these brave, persistent souls have actively engaged in preserving Henry's birthplace. Without them, a critical segment of his legacy would never have been protected.

FOREWORD

A CONVERSATION WITH ERIK AND CHRISTOPHER LOREN
EWERS CODIRECTORS OF *HENRY DAVID THOREAU*,
A THREE-PART PBS DOCUMENTARY (2026)

Ken Lizotte speaks with acclaimed filmmakers Erik and Christopher Loren Ewers about the man behind Walden Pond and his surprising legacy as a savvy, practical thinker. For over thirty years, the Ewers brothers have shared a passion for uncovering the human stories within important social issues. They believe a foundation of universal human experience is the key to relatability in our politically and socially divisive era, and they seek to create crucial public discourse through thoughtful and engaging filmmaking.

Ken: First of all, Chris and Erik, thank you for your willingness to participate in the foreword for my book. As you know, it's a unique book about Henry David Thoreau due to its focus on Henry as a business thinker, which, amazingly, is coming to market in the same time frame as your own unique documentary, the first Thoreau documentary to be broadcast nationally. So it's like we're "Thoreau cousins" of a sort!

Erik: Yes, we're really privileged that the topic of Thoreau's life came to our attention a couple of years ago and that we'll be able to kind of "preview" it for your readers. So thank you for the invitation!

Chris: The irony is that in high school, we were *not* fans of Thoreau's *Walden* despite it being assigned reading for both of us in English class. We found it too dense back then to take in, too cerebral. We just didn't understand it! But now that we're in our adulthood and have enough life experience behind us to understand Thoreau properly, taking on this project allowed his material to teach us a lot about ourselves and how to better live our lives by looking at things differently.

Ken: It was a similar awakening for me, especially as I was never assigned Henry's works in school at all. Instead he first came into my life when a close friend of mine handed me a paperback version of Henry's "Civil Disobedience" essay during the Vietnam War era. Although my book is subtitled *Business Lessons from Henry David Thoreau*, I, like many Thoreau fans, never thought of him as a business-minded person.

And yet, after this concept came to me in a flash one day, I uncovered a wealth of evidence that this aspect of his life was very much who he was, in addition to all the other facets that he has become known for. However, given your focus was much wider than mine, when and how did you also recognize that Henry was apparently more astute business-wise than the usual documentary or biography typically gave him credit for?

Erik: Early in the pages of *Walden*, Thoreau's account of how he went about building his famous cabin tells you a lot! For one thing, he kept meticulous track of his expenses, accounting for every half-penny he spent, even seeking out recycled material, such as siding from a railroad immigrant's shanty! In the end, the total cost of his little house ran to only about $20—an impressive feat even for a builder in his time. So from this, he penned the phrase "The cost of a thing is the amount of what I will call life, which is required to be exchanged for it, immediately or in the long run."

Chris: So what he called his "experiment" of living in the woods was less about being some prophetic woodsman isolated from society and much more about learning how to live the way he wanted in society. He labeled his mission an effort to live "simply" and "deliberately," but he was well aware that to accomplish that, he still had to make money. He wanted to make it [on] his own terms—in harmony with the natural world that he had come to respect and, for that matter, come to *love*. In light of this revelation, he was encouraging us to take a look at our own lives and think carefully about the value behind our own labors.

Erik: Because of that insight, Chris and I also wanted to be very careful not to dictate in the film what each viewer should learn. We decided we'd rather have everyone learn along with him, learning what he's learning *as* he's learning it. One great example of that was when Henry joined his dad's pencil-making company. I love how Henry became so interested in that venture that he volunteered to research the standard pencil-manufacturing process to potentially make this product *superior* to what was at that time . . . in the marketplace. As a result, he not only succeeded in creating a better-quality pencil but even improved the current state of pencil-making *machinery*! His curiosity and intelligence was endless, and because of that the family firm prospered throughout America, rising to the top of the heap. In our film we wanted our viewers to sense that "eureka" sensation at the same moment Henry did.

Ken: Personally, I've always thought that if Henry's success at reinventing the pencil was his only business achievement, that alone would have set his place in history.

Erik: Absolutely. And yet Henry didn't stop there, applying his scientific and mathematical intelligence to other endeavors like teaching, botany, husbandry, and, increasingly, land surveying. In that area, he both trained himself and purchased his own equipment, then proceeded to prove his ability by measuring—pro bono—the length, width, and even the depth of Walden Pond itself . . . and with remarkable accuracy! Ultimately, he became the go-to guy for surveying in and around Concord and eventually was asked by landowners and businessmen to conduct fee-paid surveys as far afield as Nantucket and Perth Amboy, New Jersey.

Chris: Concord in fact designated him its *official* surveyor. He was considered the best around.

Ken: What about Henry's literary career? Could we consider him a business success in that regard?

Erik: Was Henry a successful writer? Ha! It depends on how you look at it. He made very little money from writing during his lifetime, considering that his first published book was a failure, and his second, *Walden*, sold only moderately well while he was alive. Certainly nowhere near enough to live on.

Chris: So with such limited success, you would think he would have been miserable, right? Yet he was not. For example, he never stopped writing. In addition to his two published books and his many, many essays, he plugged away at a daily journal totaling two million words for over twenty years, a series of writings that were published only many years after he passed. Plus whatever he wrote, he obsessed over every paragraph, sentence, phrase, and word. He would not release anything until he was fully satisfied with it, which sometimes put him at odds with magazine editors and jeopardized his career.

Ken: Sounds like a true writer to me! What triggered his dedication to this at times frustrating career/business path?

Erik: The middle segment of our film series, although basically about Walden Pond, a place where he becomes rooted in both writing and nature, also recounts a trip to Maine. There Thoreau climbs Mount Katahdin, the highest mountain he can find, thinking he's going to find "God" at the top. But all he finds there is that he nearly freezes to death! At that point he has an epiphany, a combination of his experience at Walden plus Katahdin. He realizes then that the sublime in nature is all around him.

Chris: This signals him that the meadows high up on Katahdin and the meadows he knows so well in Concord are one in the same, equally beautiful. This is a huge revelation that allows his writing to just start pouring out of him in a new way, a kind of transformative, metaphorical process that he had never experienced before. Our episode ends with him declaring, "I have several more lives to live," which tells him it's time to move on, especially in the direction of writing, the career path he cares about the most.

Erik: As he so beautifully wrote, "The mass of men lead lives of quiet desperation." This is probably truer now than it was then. And it transforms our film into an *opportunity* to really apply everything that Thoreau represents to *today's* world. Because it suggests we may realize, "Wow, I've been missing out on a lot personally."

Ken: All you need to do is find your own Walden, right?

Erik: Yes! By stepping away from the endless distractions of today, you can take a different look. That seems to be what Henry is asking us to do.

To enjoy the remainder of the hour Ken spent with Erik and Chris, email Ken via ken@thoughtleading.com for a free transcript.

PREFACE

Thousands of books have been written about Henry David Thoreau since his death in 1862, from biographies and critical analyses of his writings to studies of his role in pioneering environmentalism and his contributions to philosophy, politics, social reform, and engineering.

Yet, remarkably, no single book has focused exclusively on his innovative business thinking. When I first mentioned to two of my Thoreau colleagues that I was exploring this idea, both—although familiar with Henry's work life—chuckled aloud. The very notion of Thoreau as a business expert of any sort struck them as absurd.

His dedicated fans might assume he avoided the subject entirely, preferring idyllic contemplation. Indeed, common portrayals of Henry Thoreau celebrate him as an influential thoughtleader in *nearly* every realm. During my decade as president of the Thoreau Farm Trust Board of Directors, we hosted countless events focused on Henry and his fellow transcendentalists' ideas. Everything about everything, it seemed—just not business.

I overlooked this omission for years despite my career as a writer, literary agent, and developer of business books. But one day, it struck me: What about Henry's *business mind?* Could a thinker this profound, eclectic, and deep really not have one? The more I thought about it, the more I felt compelled to investigate. What might I discover?

This exploration felt deeply aligned with Henry's own reasoning for camping out for two years, two months, and two days on the tranquil shores of nearby Walden Pond:

I went to the woods because I wished to live deliberately, to front only the essential facts of life, and see if I could not learn what it had to teach, and not, when I came to die, discover that I had not lived. I did not wish to live what was not life, living is so dear; nor did I wish to practice resignation, unless it was quite necessary. I wanted to live deep and suck out all the marrow of life, to live so sturdily and Spartan-like as to put to rout all that was not life, to cut a broad swath and shave close, to drive life into a corner, and reduce it to its lowest terms.

As a fellow Concordian, I visited the special collections at the Concord Free Public Library—mere steps away from Henry's childhood home, the boardinghouse that his mother, Cynthia Dunbar, founded and managed. With the aid of director Anke Voss and her brilliant staff, I began seeking evidence for my thesis: Had Henry contributed as profoundly to business as he had to other fields?

Before I left the library that day, I knew I was onto something. Was Henry a serious business thinker? Was he ever! The proof, to my growing delight, was everywhere.

NOTE TO THE READER

- Some quotations in this book are condensed or polished slightly for clarity and flow.

- Where historical gaps exist, some scenes are fictionalized—based on available historical information—to paint a picture of how certain interactions and developments *might* have played out. These sections will be identified by the words "*One could imagine*" or similar phrasing.

- For ease and familiarity, I refer to Henry David Thoreau throughout the book as "*Henry*," while his mentor and friend Ralph Waldo Emerson appears as "*Waldo*," as his friends and family referred to him. This is not only to simplify these repeated references but to also bring these "characters" to life. Henry, I suspect, would approve of the simplification!

- Similarly, Henry's father's pencil factory—which went through a number of name changes—is referred to simply as "Thoreau Pencils."

- Henry's direct quotations from his works in the text are set in italics.

- This book mirrors *Walden's* eighteen-chapter structure but is not a chronological biography. To ameliorate confusion, timelines of Henry's writings and life events are included in the appendices.

- Keep a sharpened #2 pencil handy for the workbook sections at the end of each chapter—a fitting tribute, since Henry himself perfected its design!

HENRY RESPONDS TO HARVARD

In 1847, Henry replied to a letter from his class secretary asking how life had been since they'd graduated from Harvard ten years before. True to form, his answer brimmed with candor:

> *I don't know whether mine is a profession, or a trade, or whatnot... It is not one but legion (so let me) give you some of the monster's heads. I am a Schoolmaster—a private Tutor, a Surveyor— a Gardener, a Farmer—a Painter. I mean a House Painter, a Carpenter, a Mason, a Day-Laborer, a Pencil-Maker, a Glass-paper Maker, a Writer, and sometimes a Poetaster... For the last two or three years I have lived in Concord woods alone, something more than a mile from any neighbor, in a house built entirely by myself.*

This book aims to expand on Henry's self-portrait, revealing how much further his eclectic skills propelled him to professional success—a significant and all too rarely acknowledged facet of Henry's legacy.

WALDEN POND.
A reduced Plan.
1846.

Scale $\frac{1}{7920}$ or 40 rods to an inch.

Area 61 acres 103 rods.
Circumference 1.7 miles.
Greatest Length 175½ rods. A
Greatest Depth 102 feet.

Railroad to Concord & Fitchburg

C

B

True Meridian

Sand-bar

Bare Peak

Wooded Peak

Profile of a Section by the line A B.

A ———————————————————————————————— B

Section C.D.

C ——————————————— D

Town

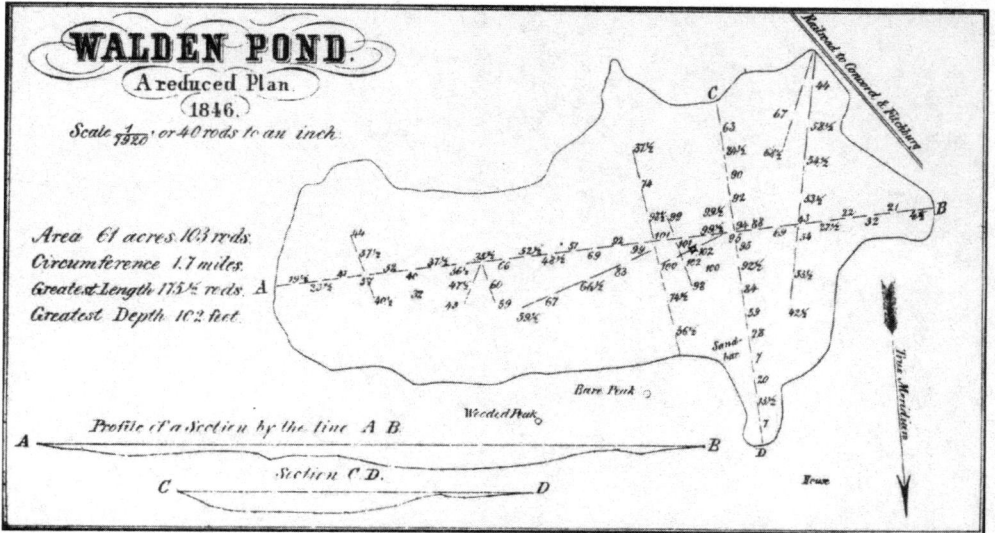

Henry's 1846 pro bono survey of Walden Pond (see chapter 8).

INTRODUCTION

When he spied the little bird's nest beside the old Indian trail along Walden Pond, one could imagine that Henry was immediately transfixed. It was late August now—its springtime inhabitants, likely a family of industrious robins, were obviously finished with it, their eggs hatched, their fledglings swooping between branches without need of parents. The nest had served its purpose.

Somehow, it had come loose from its snug perch. Perhaps a squirrel had dislodged it, or a fox in pursuit of a meal, may have knocked it harshly off its limb. However it happened, the nest now lay along one of Henry's favorite sauntering routes.

The very sight of it spurred Henry to crouch down, not touching it at first, just eyeing it all over, then fingering it ever so lightly to study it top to bottom. *What a marvel*, he mused, *what perfection! Simplicity in nature.*

He carefully brought it to eye level, marveling at its construction. Henry's next thought was to take it apart, scientifically, twig by twig—a feat of "reverse engineering" (though this term had not yet been coined). With thumb and forefinger, he delicately slipped a one-inch twig out from all the rest, noting where and how it had fit in. *Ah, Step One!*

Step Two was slowly drawing out a skinny twig of similar length from the opposite side of this astonishingly circular structure, just to see what would happen. Would the structure fall all apart? Or was it sturdier than it looked? At what point would the nest cease to be a nest, unwinding like a sweater into a muddled pile of loose threads?

The more Henry proceeded, the more perfectly constructed this nest proved to be: a seemingly haphazard jigsaw of natural ingredients, assembled without glue or nails by an architect with a tiny bird brain . . . but impeccably!

Finally, Henry laid the remnants on a bed of moss off the side of the trail, offering a silent bow of respect and wonder before sauntering along. As he strode away, he considered what he had just encountered. The lesson of the nest wasn't yet clear, but he knew it would come to him when the time was right, perhaps by dinner.

After all, to examine life was what made it worth living.

A Deeper Peek

Henry's life is most often framed through his roles as writer, environmentalist, thinker, surveyor, explorer, and activist. While informed scholars agree that these capture his best-known achievements, a closer examination reveals a far more diverse professional portfolio. As he had reported to that Harvard class secretary, he had also worked as a handyman, poet, teacher, tutor, explorer, expert marketer, builder, farmer, travel writer, public speaker, event organizer, and—most surprisingly—a successful *businessman and inventor.* Like so much else that he attempted, Henry excelled in these endeavors, often outperforming his contemporaries.

Yet his literary, environmental, and philosophical fame has overshadowed these remarkable achievements. Examining them reveals an impressive business skill set that, if on a CV today, or posted as a LinkedIn profile, might look like this:

Henry David Thoreau

Professional Achievements

Business & Innovation
- Revolutionized pencil manufacturing through European research, developing a superior formula that made Thoreau Pencils America's premier manufacturer
- Developed effective marketing broadsides and advertisements for surveying business, establishing it as the premier vendor in the region
- Harvested crops on a small farm that at times outdid the yields and profits of all competing farmers in the area

Teaching
- Co-founded, co-managed, and taught at a school for young students that implemented an unconventional curriculum (open dialogue, nature walks, science lectures) to produce independent thinkers rather than cogs in an industrial workplace
- Tutored children of educated families

Writing & Thoughtleadership
- Published two books, multiple essays, and two hundred poems, as well as a personal journal totaling two million words on such varied topics as nature, surveying, religion, philosophy, politics, travel, adventure, science, and more

- Public speaker on topics listed previously and on controversial issues of the day
- Observed and recorded plant, animal, bird, and insect life, including yearly observations that ultimately led to an annual climate change project conducted by Boston University and environmental experts still going strong today

Practical Skills
- Builder of pondside "tiny house" cabin of his own design constructed primarily from natural and recycled materials and, to keep costs down, aided by borrowed tools
- Expert accounting and management skills as evidenced in a variety of industries, including family pencil factory, private school, survey company, green bean farm, tiny house construction, handyman services, all of which turned a profit

Education
- Harvard College, Class of 1837. Studied classical languages (Latin, Greek) as well as Italian, Spanish, English, German, rhetoric, philosophy, mathematics, science, history, graduating in the top half of his class
- Informal graduate research, e.g., the science of evolution, pencil manufacturing, environmentalism, plant classification, and more

Published Works

Books

- *A Week on the Concord and Merrimack Rivers* (James Munro and Company)
- *Walden; or, Life in the Woods* (Ticknor and Fields Publishers)

Selected Essays

- "Cape Cod" in *Putnam's Monthly*
- "Slavery in Massachusetts" in *The Liberator*
- "A Yankee in Canada" in *Putnam's Monthly*
- "Walking" in *The Atlantic Monthly*
- "Ktaadn and the Maine Woods" in *The Union Magazine*
- "Resistance to Civil Government" in *Aesthetic Papers*

Sampling of Speaking Topics

- Walden: My Two Years, Two Months, Two Days Living in the Woods
- Pencil-Making Done Right
- Land Surveying with an Ethical Attitude
- Wild Apples: Where to Find Them, Keeping Them Safe in Our Fields
- Moonlight: When Night Turns to Day (video light show)
- Moose Hunting: So Much to Learn . . . and to Change! (slideshow)
- A Plea for John Brown: Mistakes We Must Not Make Again
- A Trip to the Maine Woods (slideshow)
- The Succession of Forest Trees: How They Got There, How to Keep Them Safe
- Forming a Huckleberry Party

"What an Infinite Bustle!"

Who wouldn't want to hire this guy? Or at least interview him? Or reach out to him as a consultant to help solve in-house challenges?

- Imagine him adding new credits to his LinkedIn profile every year or every month!
- Imagine a two-minute video of him on his website or YouTube channel!
- Imagine his public speaking "sizzle-reel" on a speaker's bureau website!
- Imagine the length and breadth of testimonials from satisfied customers!

Henry himself articulated his own business frame of mind this way, with comments that spoke to it directly:

- *This world is a place of business. What an infinite bustle!*
- *A man is rich in proportion to the number of things which he can afford to let alone.*
- *The cost of a thing is the amount of what I will call life which is required to be exchanged for it, immediately or in the long run.*
- *Beware of all enterprises that require new clothes.*

Despite the drumbeat of nonbusiness depictions of Henry over the decades since he left us—the hermit, the recluse, the hippie, the ne'er-do-well, the curmudgeon—the wealth of evidence of his business acumen is formidable.

BUSINESS LESSON

This world is but canvas to our imagination. Always examine with an uncensored mind to discover what works and what does not. Do not make assumptions about reality; instead pursue *evidence*. Reverse engineering can help!

Grab your favorite #2 and pencil in your own business lesson here:

_____

_____

_____

WALDEN
FOR HIRE

1

"BEGIN WITH WALDEN"

I have always endeavored to acquire strict business habits;
they are indispensable to every man.

What's amazing about the fact that so little has been written about Henry David Thoreau's business mind is that the very first chapter of his masterpiece *Walden* is titled "Economy." The proper way to begin *Walden for Hire* then is to first focus our attention there.

In fact, in my first research interview, with Mike Frederick—at the time executive director of the Thoreau Society, the premiere association for contemporary fans of Henry, whose membership spans the globe—Mike advised me to do this before I'd thought of it myself. Until Mike said it, I'd expected that my research must delve deeply into little-known corners of Thoreau scholarship populated by academics who labored selflessly in the shadows, far from the usual Henry story angles such as plants, trees, birds, animals, rivers, and, of course, his time at Walden Pond.

"Begin with chapter 1 of *Walden*," Mike said matter-of-factly, his voice quietly resonant with years of attentive dedication to Henry's ways. "That's where Henry lays out his business thinking. There's no better place to get started than there."

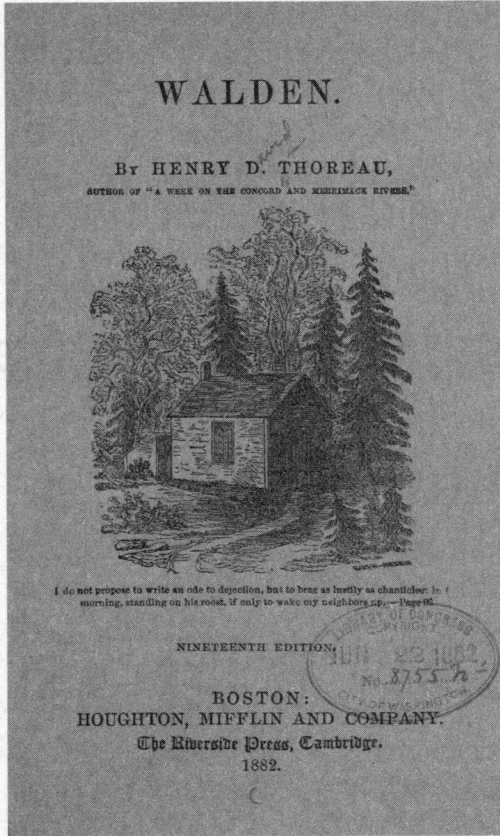

WALDEN.

By HENRY D. THOREAU,
AUTHOR OF "A WEEK ON THE CONCORD AND MERRIMACK RIVERS."

I do not propose to write an ode to dejection, but to brag as lustily as chanticleer in the
morning, standing on his roost, if only to wake my neighbors up.—Page 92.

NINETEENTH EDITION.

BOSTON:
HOUGHTON, MIFFLIN AND COMPANY.
The Riverside Press, Cambridge.
1882.

So I did what I was told, followed Mike's advice, and oh, was Mike ever so right.

Early on in the pages of "Economy," for example, Henry expresses his serious concern that life wasn't really worth living if you had to end up knocking your head against a wall, over and over, just to make even a minimal living. Too often, no matter how hard a worker works, a continuous lifestyle of falling into debt takes over, preventing such hard workers from ever fully enjoying life. Just as one's service or product must be worth another's while if it be purchased, the very labor behind it must feel similarly worthwhile, rewarding its laborer with meaning and a sense of purpose and satisfaction. Yet looking around him, in his hometown of Concord, he found very little of this.

Instead, the flip side of the work/career coin for many of those he encountered seemed to be universally accepted that work was 100% toil and 0% fulfillment, and that was that.

Thus Henry's pronouncement on this matter in *Walden* became the stuff of legend:

> *The mass of men lead lives of quiet desperation. What is called resignation is confirmed desperation. From the desperate city you go into the desperate country [where] a stereotyped but unconditional despair is concealed even under what are called the games and amusements of mankind. There is no play in them, for this comes [only] after work. But it is a characteristic of wisdom not to do desperate things.*

To reconcile this with something deep inside Henry that ate at him day and night, he found himself struggling over how to avoid such a life of depressing desperation. Where could he turn? How could he play *during* his work life, not just after his workday? He must find magic in whatever thrilled and excited him, lit his fire. But what *was* that?

And, just as important, how? As a former career consultant, I came to understand intimately a lengthy list of insights that professionals in midlife career crises would typically share with me, running the gamut from their work-related frustrations to personal delights. But the two most basic of all that have never left me are these:

1. Given a realistic opportunity to choose a job or business that is personally rewarding versus exceedingly lucrative, 90% will choose a *rewarding* work life every time.

2. Two categories of workers dominate the wide world of work, and only two: entrepreneurs and employees. And this is a dividing line that is hard to cross, I came to understand; we are either one or the other. So pay attention to which one is right for you!

For Henry, as we shall see, the answer was clear: Only the first one was personally rewarding for him, an absolute must: entrepreneur. Most of his work life would be spent here, in pursuit of how much he could achieve beyond even the boundaries of job restrictions. Which is to say that entrepreneurialism, that one-word synonym for *business owner*, was how he would handle himself *always,* even within the confines of so-called secure employment. As he put it:

I have always endeavored to acquire strict business habits [as] they are indispensable to every man.

He would prove this point, one way or another, in every work environment he would find himself. In some cases, this would lead to disaster while in others to spectacular, transformative new worlds.

"I Turned My Face to the Woods"

Looking around him, what with the world's most remarkable new technology now on the scene—the railroad!—one could imagine Henry noting that most work options seemed to hold no clear attractions for him. In the village of Concord, for example, there were general stores, livery stables, undertakers, cobblers, law offices, and repair shops, yet none of these pulled him their way. Beyond that, the railroad failed to interest him as a potential career particularly given his apprehensions about what it might mean to the world he had grown up in. Lastly, what did he actually "qualify" for anyway, whether in nearby Boston or right here in his hometown?

So, standing in the precise center of Concord village, turning slowly 360 degrees around to absorb the full impact of so much busyness, he might have ultimately stopped as he faced one dusty road out of town that pointed in a certain direction: the long road leading to the woodlands embracing Walden Pond.

Why this way? he must have wondered. Nothing was really down there, right? Surely no work to be had.

Yet the more he gazed, the more it may have made sense to him. Might he establish a "business" out past the rough roads of the village? Might he set up shop out there and produce and sell something, somewhere down in the very midst of so much wildness? Somewhere beneath the tallest pine groves and in sight of the cool Walden water and breezes, the songbirds all around, the scents of the greenery wafting up from where his feet touched the earth, how or where he couldn't know, but . . . something about it made more and more sense. He would create something there.

I have [often] thought that Walden Pond would be a good place for business, he had recently written, *and not solely on account of the railroad or the ice trade*. He was already thinking beyond the obvious, contemplating a business that might have nothing at all to do with the chug-chugging new rail transportation that had only recently begun hauling more than one hundred Bostonians each workday to the brick factory of Damon Mill (rebuilt after a fire), and perhaps forty to fifty more from the other direction, that end of the line in the country town of Fitchburg. It was these who sweated—desperately, one imagines!—through ten- to twelve-hour work shifts, six days each week, producing "domett cloth," a light wool flannel, and then at the end of an insufferably long, hot day, packing into a stuffy passenger car for the fifty-minute ride back to Boston or Fitchburg, or shorter rides to the other little towns and hamlets along either route.

As for his mention of the "ice trade," these were employees from the Concord Icehouse who walked every day to the pond to spend eight to ten hours cutting glassy squares out of the ice from an inlet now called Ice Fort Cove, then packing them into wooden "iceboxes" for transporting to houses, stores, and offices in Concord and surrounding towns.

[So] *I turned my face more exclusively than ever to the woods*, Henry wrote in *Walden, where I was better known. I determined to go onto business at once and not wait to acquire for the usual capital, using such slender means as I had already got*. He would start basically from scratch; he would visit the woods and see what emerged as a "business." But his purpose was not to live cheaply at

Walden Pond, a so-called kettle pond, which many folks, irrationally, thought had no bottom. Kettle ponds form when a block of stagnant ice detaches from a glacier that slowly melts, leaving behind a pit. Water then begins filling the depression and forming a pond or lake, taking the shape of a kettle.

No, Henry's goal was to *transact some private business with the fewest obstacles*, chiefly other people's opinions of whether he should be doing this *at all*, let alone the how or the what of all that it might become.

I was now beginning to see why Mike Frederick had directed me to Henry's first chapter. His business mind after all was emerging right at the throes of a time in his life when decisions revolving around what to do about his work life were most in doubt, most beneath the surface of his waters of confusion. Anyone else would have walked meekly across the street to this store, that office, the barber shop, the livery stables, asking, with straw hat in hand, if there might be some work available. *Any* work.

Gaining that little, even if worlds away from work he would truly love to be would at least let him end the day in ecstasy, hurrying home to burst through the screen door calling, "Ma, Pa, I got a job today!" What cause for celebration, however brief. But by morning, the reality would settle in. A job, yes, but only that. A job to help pay bills. A job to keep him busy six days a week. A job, yes—but a *life*? No.

Instead, Henry saw fit to challenge himself with a blind run at the unknown: a glance into a dark pool, a deep breath, and then the plunge. It was too deep to see just yet, but Henry's heart guided him to what surely awaited him at Walden Pond.

"The Mistake of Men in Labor"

As this business was to be entered into without the usual capital, it may not be easy to conjecture where those means, that will still be indispensable to every such undertaking, were to be obtained.

Any brand-new enterprise, Henry wrote in "Economy," must be somehow funded if only to keep the founder(s) going until their start-up could begin bringing in revenue for salaries and living expenses for both themselves and their employees, and to attract more and more customers whose purchases would support the company's various costs of doing business, thereby at a minimum breaking even, and to ultimately reap a steady actual profit that could grow until this new company could be confidently labeled financially healthy and thus a success.

But as Henry's start-up funding consisted of only the scant dollars he carried in his pocket, he would need to devise a system that differed significantly from, say, the conventional methodology for funding a new factory or railroad or even a general store. Since he was uncertain what his new business would even do, be, produce, or offer, he needed to think through a system all his own. He began by observing the results of business and work-life decisions all around him. For example, how did the typical farmer or laborer meet their own needs, the so-called necessaries of life? And what was their plan for sustaining needed income throughout their whole lives?

Henry saw most men laboring under a *mistake*—they had become *serfs of the soil*, born with *inherited encumbrances*, eventually *plowed into the soil for compost*. Burdened by mortgages or rent, family expenses, and endless needs, the typical farmer or day laborer could never catch up, forever chasing life's necessities yet never quite grasping them.

Thus the *coarse labors* take over so fully that life's *finer fruits cannot be plucked by them*. Days were consumed by work, nights by worry, until the cycle consumed their entire lives. *It is a fool's life*, Henry proclaimed, *something they will discover "when they get to the end of it, if not before."* To Henry, there had to be a better way.

Yet this *mistake of men in labor* stemmed from a deeper fallacy: an attitude that there in fact *wasn't* a better way. How else to attain the necessaries of life but to work and work and then work some more? Six days of drudgery with one for rest was the norm all around him. He observed it everywhere—in the village of Concord, its surrounding farms, and even among those who squatted along the shores of Walden Pond.

But what, Henry asked, if a six-day week was *not* the norm? What if the norm was turned on its head, that a farmer/laborer worked only *one* day a week, leaving the other six days for pleasure, discovery, reading, appreciation of nature, writing, society, music . . . adventure! How could one attain such a reversal given the dauntless challenges imposed by the necessaries of life?

It came to him one day all in a rush. Exactly where he was standing or sitting or walking, or even—gasp—working, right then and there it came to him, spilling onto a page in one of his seven drafts of *Walden*: "Our life is frittered away," he wrote, "by detail. Then—think, think . . . Ahh . . . yes . . . YES! Simplicity! Yes, simplicity, yes . . . simplicity, simplicity, simplicity!"

An honest man has hardly need to count more than his ten fingers or in extreme cases he may add his ten toes, and lump the rest. Simplicity, simplicity, simplicity! I say, let your affairs be as two or three, and not a hundred or a thousand. Then, a few lines later, as if he just cannot say it enough, or has perhaps decided it to be instructive to simplify the very word *simplicity* itself, he adds "Simplify, simplify," elaborating, *Instead of three meals a day, if it be necessary eat but one; instead of a hundred dishes, five; and reduce other things in proportion.*

By George, he may very well have got it! If the necessaries of life are the problem, attack the problem! Find a way to tackle them differently.

The Necessaries of Life

So, having identified a solution, Henry's next step required pinning down the problem. What in fact were, precisely, the necessaries of life? And how formidable were they? Granted, each working man faced a customized version of his particular struggle with the necessaries, but what might some tailored responses to the necessaries look like? And ultimately how would Henry also do battle with those necessaries facing his own goals and dreams?

Again, deeply thinking it through, Henry self-brainstormed about how to right what for many was a continually sinking ship:

Necessary #1: Food & Drink. One must eat of course and eating either costs money or requires time to grow and/or hunt. Henry opined one might eat fewer meals and perhaps with fewer options. Rarely, for example, did he eat meat, and he also consumed fish in moderation as well as beans, rice, and vegetables. Consequently he has been labeled a reducetarian, that is, he consumed reduced portions of his meals and drank only water (no coffee, alcohol, milk, wine, or tea). Thus, only a little expense for food and no expense at all for drink.

Henry: *There is a difference between eating and drinking for strength and from mere gluttony. To the bison it is a few inches of palatable grass on the prairie with water to drink.*

Necessary #2: Shelter. Henry fixated on the "encumbrances" brought on by building, renting, or purchasing a multi-room house and all that such a structure entailed. His own solution would come to be a one-room cabin or "house" (as he chose to call it) that he would build himself on the shores of Walden Pond. This decision vastly reduced the cost and troublesomeness of a larger domicile.

Henry: *The great necessity for our bodies is to keep warm. With adequate shelter, we retain our own internal heat.*

Necessary #3: Clothing. How much clothing does one actually need? How many coats, pairs of shoes, pantaloons, hoop skirts? His own wardrobe was quite modest, including patches on his pants and shirts so as not to need to be always buying new ones. Sewing patches onto his clothing kept the cost of this necessary in check.

Henry: *What pains we take, not only with our food, clothing, and shelter, but with our beds, which are our night clothes.*

Necessary #4: Fuel. Warmth is essential, Henry admits, especially in the freezing climate of winter in New England. For Henry, as for most of his fellow farmers and laborers, this demanded chopping wood daily for stoking a home hearth (or multiple hearths in a larger house). Keeping the fires burning at least until time to sleep with a thick, homemade quilt would maintain one's warmth from bedtime until morning!

Henry: *The luxuriously rich are not simply kept comfortably warm by fuel, but unnaturally hot; as I implied before, they are cooked.*

Necessary #5: Exercise:* This one, and the next two, were not on Henry's list as outlined in the second half of "Economy." But Henry most definitely tackled this one as well without spending even one US penny due to his typical four-hour "saunters." Throughout both Concord and Walden Woods, and literally every day, he would walk, walk, walk. Plus in summer months he would swim in Walden or another pond, and in winter skate across these same, now fully icy waters. He would also canoe down the Sudbury, Assabet, and Concord Rivers most of the year and, for "strength training," chop wood, lift and carry heavy wooden beams, push up the sides of barns and newly rebuilt houses, and haul up sections of roofs for all manner of constructions. He did, however, believe most in walking, which he viewed as not just exercise but an opportunity for new adventures.

Henry: *If you would get exercise, go in search of the springs of life.*

Necessary #6: Social interaction:† Though Henry didn't write about this one as a necessary of life, today we have come to learn of its

---

* No one in those days ran for sport or health, as we do now, no road races, marathons, or one-hundred-yard dashes. With one exception: Louisa May Alcott as a teen loved running at top speed down Concord streets, all by herself, any time of day, in traditional dress and over-the-ankle leather shoes. It may not have been uncommon to hear someone cry, "There goes Louey!"

† Henry loved to debate, challenge, converse with, and pick the brains of all manner of people,

importance for mental and emotional health. Being sociable and having at least a few close friends affords an additional means of maintaining a long and healthy life, according to multiple recent studies. Henry was a natural at this, connecting with Concordians of all stripes and interacting with them robustly. He even regularly sauntered into town to chat and dine and gossip with both townsfolk and his immediate family. Thus it might not have occurred to him that this too deserved to be rated a necessary.

Henry: *I had three chairs in my house: one for solitude, two for friendship, three for society.*

Necessary #7: Sleep. We all need a good night's sleep! Though Henry said little about this, he did comment now and then on the soothing chirps or croaks of nature outside his cabin—birds and frogs especially—likening their sweet, cheerful evocations to inducements toward deep sleep and peace. He appreciated waking up early from such restful sleeps to appreciate the arrival of a new day.

Henry: *To be awake is to be alive!*

Influence of Mom and Dad

In so much of the Thoreau literature today, there is brief mention of Henry's parents and brief info about who they were, where they came from, what jobs they held and/or businesses they owned or started. Mainly this seems to be reflective of the scant reporting on them in Henry's writing.

Yet as I have pored through so much of the literature that tells us about Henry and his thinking, pursuits, wanderings, and attitudes, I've grown increasingly curious about what effect each of his parents may have had on him, positive or negative.

---

especially railroad workers, fishermen, blacksmiths, freed slaves, neighbors, best friends, lighthouse keepers, etc., in Concord or while traveling to other villages and farms.

Though long before our current age of helicopter parents, one has to wonder about his parents' reactions to Henry's daily decisions, such as his four-hour daily explorations of Concord and environs, and his decisions to choose a lifestyle surrounded by pine trees and critters and wildlife of all kinds. One wonders too their reaction when he would hide away in his attic apartment studying nature, religion, politics, philosophy, what-have-you, then emerge to announce a new thought or insight. Were his parents engaged with him at these moments or annoyed or impressed by him? Were they proud of him or were they checked out, perhaps distracted by other aspects of their own lives? The chief point, to me, is that we just do not know.

Yet here was this renaissance wunderkind whom they chose, out of all their four extraordinary children, to invest in sending to college at a time when college was nowhere near the big deal it is today. Back then in many ways higher education was a playground chiefly for rich kids, especially rich *boys,* and, if lucky, a climb up the status ladder to an elevated other world whose inhabitants all grew into lawyers and doctors and managers and bankers and ministers and—heavens! rarely, but yes occasionally—poets and writers!

For most families, inserting a son or daughter into one's "family business," be it a farm, general store, haberdashery, or funeral parlor, was the norm. Jobs in those days were hard to come by, more so when a recession was in play, or a "panic," as it used to be called. In fact, in the very year that Henry graduated from Harvard, just such an economic storm was raging, known in today's history books officially as the Panic of 1837.

Henry, however, was special to his parents, or so it seems. And as with Henry and all three of his siblings, their parents John and Cynthia were special as well. For one thing, both were entrepreneurs! John Thoreau Sr., despite a period spent in Boston as a teacher and then later for a short time as a Concord farmer, came to spend far more of his life as founder and keeper of a general store. Though not always wildly successful—he was known to be hesitant to ask regular customers to pay up their burgeoning outstanding bills—he was nonetheless successful enough to keep his family fed for many years, first in Chelmsford, a small town about ten miles from Concord, and later in Concord itself.

Ultimately his claim to fame was as a pencil manufacturer, which he did manage successfully for many years, or at least as successfully as one could in an industry whose products were not always all they were cracked up to be. Generally considered an improvement on the age-old writing implements of quill and ink, pencils were viewed as a sort of high-level technology despite unpredictable consistency leading to messy or unreadable execution. Yet John managed to thrive as one of America's better producers of this new tool and thus his business was at least minimally successful.

As for Cynthia, she founded a boardinghouse in Concord where her family of six also lived. Her own mother, Mary Dunbar, had been an entrepreneur as well, founding and running a licensed tavern after inheriting from her husband one-third of a farmhouse in Concord. Referred to in those days as a "widow's third," signifying Mary was prohibited, under common law, to inherit more than one-third of any real estate holdings, Cynthia grew up the child of a mother who would not let even the most traumatic or unfair challenges stop her from succeeding.

Perhaps that's why, in her "pro bono" life, discriminatory legal roadblocks of this sort led Cynthia to an activist lifestyle in the women's anti-slavery movement, spending much time and energy volunteering (secretly) for the underground railroad. Hiding fugitive slaves in need of a night's rest at her boardinghouse on their way to Montreal or other sections of Canada, Cynthia risked prison time should authorities discover what she was up to. But she took big chances anyway and, as far as we can tell, was never caught or arrested.

So what do we have in terms of a profile of Henry's parents? Obviously, both were risk-takers, self-organizers, unafraid of challenges, able to think their way through problems, likely personable enough to negotiate their way to business growth, reasonably adept at marketing, at least adequately adept at sales. This, then, starts to add up to a couple who understood how to achieve business success and could ride the up-and-down waves of typical business hills and valleys.

They must then have handled Henry with a long leash. One can imagine them discussing him with each other like so:

JOHN: "Ah, now he wants to go live in the woods? Well, okay then, let's let him try."

CYNTHIA: "We'll see how long he lasts but . . . if I know Henry, he may just pull it off!"

With such a mindset, they possibly encouraged him, brainstormed with him, offered advice when he asked for it, and coached him, again and again, and in the end wished him all the best.

And when he fell on his face, they'd pick him up, dust him off, and push him back out again toward whatever might be his latest stretch goal and adventure.

CYNTHIA: "So he wants to be a writer, does he? A poet no less! There's a very hard life!"

JOHN: "But when Henry sets his mind to it, he can often work miracles."

CYNTHIA: "That's so, all right. Let's see how he does!"

HENRY FACTS

Their farmhouse, by the way, would two hundred years later be designated a historical site due to its legacy as Henry's birthplace. Though only the east side of the house was allowed to pass down to Cynthia's mom, that relatively small portion provided space for Henry's birth until the family was ready to move to larger quarters in Concord eight months later. Thoreau Farm today is open to visitors as a historical house dedicated to Henry's commitment to learning, social justice, writing, and developing new ideas.

Q&A WITH MIKE FREDERICK, FORMER
EXECUTIVE DIRECTOR OF THE THOREAU SOCIETY

What would you say if someone asked you what Henry did "for a living"?
Poet, essayist, writer, lecturer, tutor, schoolteacher, consultant, proprietor of a pencil business (J. Thoreau & Son), proprietor of a surveying business (Concord's library has 165 of his surveys catalogued. He laid out town plans for Perth Amboy, NJ). He also began cartographic work on the Lake Champlain region. He experimented with farming and building.

How would you characterize Henry's attitude toward "work"?
Once you've acquired the necessities, there is no need to acquire more.

What was Henry able to do well in a work-related area and/or accomplish that you envy?
He seemingly had been able to answer his "big why." He seemingly had limitless energy in pursuit of his big why. When he came to die, he apparently said, "Now comes good sailing." His friends and family commented on how beautifully he accepted his life (death being the acceptance of life). Rather than envy, I prefer to aspire to.

What was/were Henry's weakness(es) when it came to work/ career/ business?
I would hire him. He was fastidious, trustworthy. Ralph Waldo Emerson trusted him to look after his household, wife, and children while he toured Europe. Thoreau opposed a textile-based economy reliant on slavery. He was superlatively ethical and uncompromising in this regard.

What would most surprise people today about Henry's work/ career/business life that is not in the popular image of his life and persona?

That he wasn't a loafer.

BUSINESS LESSON

A man is rich in proportion to the number of things he can afford to let alone. Our lives are top-heavy with what used to be called keeping up with the Joneses. Houses, cars, expensive smartphones, travel to distant lands, Broadway theater tickets, dinners in lavish restaurants . . . the list goes on and on. Henry's world bore down with similar pressures, so Henry's reaction was to advise keeping your expenses to a minimum. To the extent you can succeed in that, the world around you may open up to a life of less pressure and debt and more pleasure. It's a tough nut to crack . . . but Henry managed to pull it off!

Grab your favorite #2 and pencil in your business lesson here:

_____

_____

_____

2

HENRY DISCOVERS
HIS DREAM CAREER

A Winter's Morning

First in the dusky dawn he sends abroad,
His early scout, his emissary, smoke,
The earliest, latest pilgrim from the roof,
To feel the frosty air, inform the day,
And while he crouches still beside the hearth,
Nor musters courage to unbar the door,
It has gone down the glen with the light wind,
And o'er the plain, unfurled its venturous wreath . . .

U pon graduation from Harvard College in 1837, Henry's first impulse regarding starting his own business or developing a "dream" career was to seek out an occupation not only challenging but formidable. The obvious target might have been teaching, since this was a "real" job at a time when jobs of any kind were hard to come by, given the economic recession causing panic all around.

Yet Henry being Henry, he allowed himself enough slack to follow his inner compass. That meant an occupation where he might exercise his brain as fully as his body and engage his emotional self as well. Sensitivity was at his core in league with the beauty and bounty of the natural world, so what could he choose that would also challenge this aspect of who he was?

One day the answer came clear to him—how, we do not know—yet it appears to have been a rather obvious vision given his compulsion to spend so much of his time both out of doors and within himself. In his essay "Walking" (published posthumously as a separate book) he proclaims without hesitation, referring to himself in the third person:

> *He would be a poet who could impress the winds and streams into his service, to speak for him; who nailed words to their primitive senses, as farmers drive down stakes in the spring, which the frost has heaved.*

A poet! Was this a practical choice? All that education at Harvard College, and the expense of it all—$55 a year tuition!—not to mention the *time* spent and the struggles to imbibe Cicero and Homer and Hesiod. Poetry! How could this dream ever come to life?

In Henry's time, as now, poets were low on the ladders of recognition, income, satisfaction, and opportunity. But as has always been true with business and career goals, from the difficulty of the Panic of 1837 right on up to our present day, this earliest career phase was basically touch and go, raising fundamental questions:

- Where to start?
- *How* to start?
- With what strategy might one develop a following that would support the work life of a poet?
- Finally, how to build a following of enthusiastic readers?

In so many ways, of course, these very questions that Henry-the-now-and-future-poet needed to resolve were identical to those facing any other budding business, say a manufacturing firm, construction company, retail store, medical practice, law firm, and so forth. Most career coaches worth their salt will advise that landing a job for oneself or starting a solo professional service requires, bottom line, precisely the same action plan as that of building a "business." The only difference in the case of the job seeker is that the end goal is to acquire *one* client and only one, one customer, one "patron" willing to pay an ongoing fee, also known as a paycheck. In other words, only *one* is needed! One very major client/customer, of course, but only one, nonetheless.

And as with a "real" business, sustainability is the key, the capability to make one's living (i.e., meet payroll, year after year, not to mention make a profit!). For most writers, poets, artists, and the like, the goal would be slightly higher than that, perhaps two or three or maybe half a dozen of very, *very* major client/customers, in the form of publishers and/or literary journals and/or magazines, but here too the purpose would be sustainability as a result of continuous income from enough targeted paying customers to keep Henry the poet busy.

For any creative professional, this is the hard part, and within this specialized grouping, poets face the toughest test of all, given their lower demand among the reading public. Consider how things played out for even the most successful poets in days gone by:

POET CASE STUDY #1: Emily Dickinson

Dickinson lived all her life in her family's home, toiling away throughout her working years on nearly 1,800 poems, only ten of which were published in her lifetime. But posthumously she is now celebrated as one of the United States' foremost poets. Without the lifelong support of her family in their Amherst, Massachusetts, mansion, however, income obstacles would have surely derailed her literary passion and achievements.

POET CASE STUDY #2: Robert Frost

Likewise, Robert Frost achieved similar honors years later, including being dubbed the most esteemed American poet of the twentieth century. He received the Pulitzer Prize for poetry four times, while his poems yielded lines that became indelible in American culture, including "miles to go before I sleep" and "I took the road less traveled."

Yet throughout much of his earlier life, Frost constantly struggled with earning sufficient income despite the growing appeal of his poetry throughout his adult years. To make ends meet, he tried, at different times, farming and teaching school, but neither proved financially successful for him. At age forty, he had still not published a single book of poems (considered a must for a truly successful poet) and had only a handful of poems published in magazines.

Around this midlife period, Frost decided to relocate his family to England in the hopes that success might finally show up for him there. Fortunately, the risk paid off, and he won a London publisher's endorsement in the form of (finally!) a published book of many of his most cherished poems. That success was then followed by another, second collection of his poems, putting Frost at long last on a fast track with not only publishers and magazines seeking out his work but readers, fans, and followers as well. Before long, he returned to the United States, where he was met with acclaim from an adoring, growing public who from then on could never again get enough of him. Near the end of his life, at the age of eighty-eight, Frost was invited to share his poem "The Gift Outright" at the inauguration of John F. Kennedy in January 1963 on a freezing cold and blustery day on the steps of the US Capitol.

POET CASE STUDY #3: Walt Whitman

Meanwhile back in Henry's time, Walt Whitman Jr., two years younger than Henry, was a basically unknown poet struggling to make ends meet most of his life, in his case by serving as editor, journalist, teacher, and government clerk. Many of these jobs, when he could land one, proved temporary, a frustrating reality he couldn't seem to shake.

At age thirty-five, he finally struck a bit of gold with a self-financed collection of his poems titled *Leaves of Grass*, which, although its first edition was derided and hated, and thus financially a flop, ultimately was met with enthusiasm and admiration by its later edition readers. Then came his tribute to Abraham Lincoln, "O Captain! My Captain!" after Abe's assassination, which added to Whitman's reputation as one of America's newest and most influential poets.

Yet that lack of steady income cycle seemed to always return for this "father of free verse." Still struggling financially during the latter stage of his life, he received a final boost with the publication of a volume titled *The Poems of Walt Whitman* alongside a revised version of *Leaves of Grass*. Especially in England, and in the United States as well, a deep appreciation of Whitman ultimately settled in to solidify him as an American literary great, and with that, book royalties translated into steady income.

POET CASE STUDY #4: Henry Wadsworth Longfellow

On the flip side of all these acclaimed poets' financial struggles, Henry Wadsworth Longfellow, a contemporary of Henry's, took the stage with a different story to tell. Longfellow's trajectory as a poet was smoother and steadier than the others'. Publishing forty poems even before he graduated from Bowdoin College in 1825, he then went on to teach at Bowdoin until spring 1837, when he took a position at Harvard, where Henry, in his senior year, could experience Longfellow's lectures on Germanic poetry.

In 1854, he was flush enough to quit teaching altogether and concentrate fully on his poetry from age forty-seven on. His most famous poems are still read and studied today, including "The Song of Hiawatha," "Tales of a Wayside Inn," and "Paul Revere's Ride." Income was basically never a sore subject in Longfellow's life, proving the exception to the rule.

The Dial

What was hoped to be America's first great literary magazine, *The Dial* did not fare well with its premiere issue. Founded and printed in Concord in April 1840, the driving force behind *The Dial* was Ralph Waldo Emerson, and among those literary lights he singled out for a personal invitation to participate was, of course, Henry, his young friend and fellow Concordian.

Waldo had met Henry only recently—the details are lost to history—but seemed to see a lot of promise in him early on and chose to quietly position himself as Henry's mentor. As such, he encouraged Henry to submit to *The Dial* whatever he wished, prompting Henry to submit two pieces, one a prose essay, "Aulus Persius Flaccus," and the other his poem entitled "Sympathy." Though Margaret Fuller, whom Waldo hired to serve as *The Dial*'s editor, was not wildly enthusiastic about Henry's poem, she agreed to publish it nonetheless, labeling it "good enough to save a whole bad number." But despite this dubious "endorsement," Henry was at least on the starting line of his ambition to be accepted as a poet.

Alas, public criticism started to pour in upon publication of *The Dial*'s debut issue, and nothing seemed able to counter the onslaught once it had begun. Henry's "Sympathy" also garnered negative press although Margaret Fuller defended its inclusion. But as time went on, the unceasing bad reactions took their toll such that Fuller chose not to publish Henry's next entry in *The Dial*'s follow-up edition.

Fortunately, due to Waldo's vigorous advocacy of Henry's work, however, Henry did make the third issue of *The Dial* in January 1841, so, in some ways, it looked as though the newbie poet was off and running. But good times for Henry's poetry career were not quite yet to be.

Looking toward upcoming issues later that year, Henry worked up an essay called "The Service" and a new poem "A Walk to Wachusett." Fuller rejected both. Her reasoning however was not that Henry was a "bad" essayist or poet. Instead, she felt that what he was attempting as a writer had no precedent or equal, explaining to him that he was breaking new ground. Due to his writing career being still in the throes of a learning-curve stage, he hadn't yet developed the skill set, Fuller determined, to get these to the finish line. In the end, Fuller accepted only two more of his poems for publication in *The Dial*, "Sic Vita" and "Friendship," totaling just four in all after two years of trying.

Laura Dassow Walls, author of *Thoreau: A Life*, explained it this way: "A lesser writer would have been discouraged. But Fuller's earlier point, that his talent was far greater than his execution, was not lost on Thoreau. He was a genius, no doubt, but had yet to learn his craft. This was precisely the lesson Thoreau needed to hear."

Even so, the near future held its share of challenges. Although Fuller published more of Henry's work in subsequent issues, she also continued to reject other pieces. Then in early 1844, Waldo sadly had to report that funding had run out for *The Dial*. Nowhere near enough subscriptions or donations had been coming in to keep it in business. So the April 1844 issue of *The Dial* would be its last.

For Henry, this meant leaving the nest and seeking publication elsewhere. To his surprise and joy, he soon found favor in other publications, including *The Liberator*, *Graham's Magazine*, *The Union*, and *Aesthetic Papers*. On the downside, however, these wins were few and far between, an average of only one per year, certainly nowhere near the level of income that he would need to keep on keeping on.

So as would be true with any standard business, Henry next faced an emotional "bankruptcy" coupled with a financial one, which sent his poetry dreams tumbling into oblivion. It seemed time to look elsewhere and to set his sights on a very different career path. A true business, after all, is one that makes a profit, whereas businesses that fail to earn profits year after year become legally labeled a hobby. Since Henry refused to give up on his inner drive to write more poems, it appeared that poetry would be relegated to that secondary status. Though *hobby* was not a word that Henry dwelt upon, his genuine passion for this endeavor prevented him from stopping himself from composing poems for literally the rest of his life. Hobby or no, he would soldier on.

Jeffrey S. Cramer, however, notes in his brilliant compendium of Henry's works, *The Portable Thoreau*, that although Henry did continue to write poems to the end of his life, there would come a time in the later years when this endeavor would begin to fade, little by little. Cramer explains that most of the approximately two hundred poems Henry wrote were created before he closed up his experiment at Walden Pond years before his death. "Whether the scant number of poems written in his later years stemmed from the natural outgrowth of his understanding that, as Emerson had written, it was not 'metres, but a metre-making argument that makes a poem,' or whether he realized that his prose composed more of the true essence of poetry than his verse ever could, is not made clear from any record that Thoreau left behind," Cramer writes. But whatever the case, he reports that by the mid-1850s Henry had all but fallen off the poetry wagon.

Q&A: JEFFREY S. CRAMER, AUTHOR OF *THE PORTABLE THOREAU*

What would you say if someone asked you what Henry did "for a living"?
I'm tempted to say that Thoreau "lived" for a living. That his purpose—and so many of us sadly define our lives by our jobs—was to live the best life possible in the limited time allowed to any human on Earth, and to experience joy.

On the other hand, the real answer must be: Thoreau was a writer for a living! Not necessarily because he made much money (he didn't), but if you're talking about "a living" as that which sustains us, then that had to be, pure and simply, writing.

Do you wish Henry had spent more time in one endeavor or another?
I don't. Every endeavor added to his worldview, so whether he was teaching or surveying or doing manual labor or lecturing, it all added

up to how he viewed the world. So no, I would not have suggested he do one thing over another, as it would have changed his perspective and we would have seen a slightly different Thoreau—not necessarily better or worse, but different.

What was Henry able to do well in a work-related area and/or accomplish that you envy?
I think he had a very good work ethic—whatever task he was doing to earn some needed money, he did well and seriously. His surveying, as an example, was extremely precise and well carried out, not rushed or careless. So even if he wished to be doing something else, he still did what he needed to do in the way that it needed to be done.

What should people know about Henry in relation to work/career/ business that they by and large do not know today?
That he did actually work. People think he didn't because he didn't have a nine-to-five job or career. But if you look at what he did, he worked a lot: He was a teacher. Work! He was a surveyor. Work! He was a naturalist. Walking the woods and exploring was his work! He was a writer. Work! He was a lecturer. Work! He did manual labor. Work! He worked in the family pencil factory. Work!

What would most surprise people today about Henry's work/ career/business life that is not in the popular image of his life and persona?
That if you look at him as a writer primarily, he had confidence in the success of his work, preparing essays for posthumous publication and continuing with his journals long after he would ever have use for them. He knew his works would be read in the future. So he didn't measure his success as a writer by how many copies he sold or how much he earned.

HENRY FACTS

Fees Henry earned for his prose works should also be deemed fees earned for any poems inserted within them as well. In this sense, he actually did achieve his dream to become an established, successful professional poet, especially as his poems are still published in various formats today.

BUSINESS LESSON

A grain of gold will gild a great surface but not so much as a grain of wisdom. Too much time, effort, and frustration throughout one's *entire life* simply to "make a living"—a contradictory choice of words, in Henry's view—was just not worth it. Find a way around it somehow, maybe via settling into a job or business that fills you with purpose, or, failing that, spend as much free time as possible on hobbies that you passionately enjoy. Seek to learn, gain insights, and be fulfilled rather than struggling only to "get rich."

Grab your favorite #2 and pencil in your business lesson here:

_____

_____

_____

3

A WORTHWHILE
COMPROMISE

What does education often do?
It makes a straight-cut ditch of a free,
meandering brook.

Some years before poetry began showing once and for all that it was increasingly unlikely to deliver Henry's dream career, a queasy realization had begun to sink in that his college degree from venerable Harvard was also failing to carry with it any great hopes of serious remuneration. Poetry right out of Harvard was certainly not the ticket back then, particularly in light of the burgeoning Panic of 1837.

So Henry embarked on a campaign to look near and far for a "real job" with the goal of locating and landing an alternative career, mayhap something that might offer a measure of fulfillment *and* prosperity as he continued, in the background of his mind, to maintain poetry as his ultimate goal.

One such real job did leap out at him immediately, something he had experienced as rewarding only a year or so ago and a thing he had proven to be quite capable at, something that was working for Longfellow, so why not for him too.

Teaching! *Yes, let me take a serious run at teaching*, Henry must have thought, especially now with "undergraduate degree" under his belt. And in the teaching profession, a college degree would actually mean something. What a grand opportunity to enjoy the best of two worlds!

Not that teaching would ever erase poetry as his primary goal. Robert Richardson Jr. noted in his book *Henry Thoreau: A Life of the Mind* that "Henry never thought of [teaching] as his life's work. What he really wanted to do was write. And at age twenty, what [he] really wanted to write was poetry." But that couldn't happen immediately, Henry knew. Getting from here to there required busting through a series of stumbling blocks that would take time to do. But teaching might provide the solution, freeing up time to write while nailing down a temporary financial solution. *First Longfellow*, Henry may have thought, *then me*!

As is still true today, a teaching position suggested a worthwhile compromise. Think of modern-day teacher/writers who have made it work, luminaries like T. S. Eliot, Mary Oliver, Maya Angelou, Robert Pinsky. So yes, this could actually work.

On the other hand, for Henry, once fresh out and through the gates of Harvard Yard, the timing couldn't have been worse. In the very year that he graduated, America got slammed with the Panic of 1837, a depression that reduced job opportunities and caused banks to fail and foreign investments to decline. Fortunately, however, unlike other college graduates that year, Henry had already acquired some experience in the teaching profession, having spent six weeks of his junior year teaching seventy grammar-school students a variety of subjects in a one-room schoolhouse in Canton, Massachusetts, a small town south of Boston.

Moreover, his path there and what happened after his arrival would yield ramifications for other aspects of Henry's career. Harvard had enacted a ruling that encouraged students to take one term off so they might earn extra money for their families (the Panic was coming!) by teaching at a nearby school. As a result, Henry connected with Reverend Orestes Augustus Brownson, pastor of the First Unitarian Church in Canton, who quickly let Harvard know that this young man seemed to be just what his Canton pupils needed.

To settle into Canton, Henry bunked at Brownson's home. The Reverend was a charismatic, idea-full, progressive activist who urged Henry to take up the study of German during his summer in town and to commit even more study to the language in his senior year at Harvard. What Brownson was aiming for was to convince Henry to "study the language in earnest as a vital channel of transcendental truths from abroad," according to George T. Comeau, writing in the *Canton Citizen*.

More than that, the picture that Laura Walls paints in her book is that "this was Henry's first encounter with a free-range intellectual whose ideas snapped and crackled, who moved easily in the circles of the great and the near great. His term with Brownson broke the spell of Havard."

Comeau elaborates that when, in a letter following his Canton teaching gig, "Henry refers to his time in Canton as 'the morning of a new Lebenstag,' he is giving credit to Brownson for raising his interest in philosophy and metaphysical poetry. Within (an illuminating) year of spending time with Brownson, Thoreau saw his vocation as leading the life of a poet and drinking in the 'soft influences and sublime revelations of nature.'" A lot to unpack there!

Beyond the obvious life-changing influence of Henry's six weeks in Canton, the experience also left him with some real-life street cred teaching in a public school. During the Panic, this would prove valuable after graduating a year later and gathering his college clothes, books, and sheepskin to board a stagecoach for the two-hour trip back to Concord. Though brief, it did give him a leg up on his competition, although job offers did not exactly come roaring in right after graduation. This was true despite his reaching out to friends and contacts for help. Try as they might, none of his connections yielded many serious considerations for Henry's services even with opportunities popping up beyond the borders of Concord, as far away as Maine, for example.

It got so bad that Henry began racking his brain for whatever non-teaching job leads he might be able to find, though satisfactory ideas were few and far between. Concord after all was, besides farming, a mill town, featuring a paper mill, sawmill, grist mill, and textile mill, to name a few. So maybe go work in a mill? Didn't feel right for a college grad now, did it? But if that's what it takes, well . . .

So Henry must have kept wondering, and waiting, and asking . . . until one day when an actual teaching opportunity suddenly presented itself right there in—guess where?—Concord! The amazing once-in-a-lifetime opportunity seemed to spring up out of nowhere, staring Henry in the face!

"We'd very much like you to join our faculty at the Concord Centre School," Barzillai Frost of the Concord School Committee is reported to have told him one day. "Would you be interested in a position right here in your hometown?"

Henry could not hold back his excitement! His preference would of course be to land a position in his hometown, as he had always felt quite lucky to have been born in Concord. So immediately expressing positive interest and enthusiasm, he inquired about the details of the position. "Well, the salary is $500 per year," he was told, placing him among the top government income earners in all of Concord.

Frost also assured him that reforms put in place a few years before now permitted Concord teachers to bypass the age-old conventional approach to disciplining students through corporal punishment. This was a great relief to Henry, who had been ready to insist that he would not be willing to "flog" his students. Thus he was excited to accept the job, preferring to discipline via some form of moral persuasion or personal embarrassment instead. Corporal punishment was not his style.

Fit to Teach

Once in the "master's chair," however, Henry immediately began to struggle with all the negative forces this seemingly sweet new "opportunity" forced upon him. For one thing, equipment such as maps were few and far between, and very little paint (if any!) adorned the walls. The woodstove heating system worked only erratically, causing attendance to fall to minimal on colder days and months. And discipline—oh yes . . . discipline!—proved continually needed to keep fifty or more boys and girls (but especially boys!) in check while in the same classroom.

As was the case with other educational reformers of the time, the elimination of corporal punishment as an option meant that Henry needed to impart discipline some other way. For Henry, merely communicating why outlandish behavior was unacceptable often gave them pause or persuaded them to behave. For the most part, during his first week and part of his second, such disciplinary tactics seemed to work.

But late in Henry's second week, Deacon Nehemiah Ball, the senior member of the school committee, stopped in to evaluate how Henry was doing, taking a seat in the back of the room. According to various accounts, it didn't go well! When Henry did not comply with Ball's preferred "corporal chastisement" methods, despite what Henry had been told, Ball pulled him aside to *order* Henry to start flogging unruly students lest wildness and discipline run amok and end up ruling the day. Ball had apparently not gotten the memo!

What Henry did next, Walls writes, changed his life forever. "He couldn't actually flog anyone—he didn't even own a cowhide," she tells us, "but he did possess a ferule, and that day he used it," calling up a number of students—historical accounts range from two to thirteen or more—then thrashing them on the wrists with enough force to send them back to their desks in enough pain that they remembered this day for the rest of their lives.

Hating what he had done, Henry apparently decided then and there that he could not go on. At the end of the class day, he stopped by Ball's office and resigned. On only his tenth day at work, he was through.

"Next day he returned to tell his students that punishing with force went against his conscience," Walls writes, and for that reason "he wouldn't keep school any longer, if that was the way he had to do it."

Later that night in his attic bedroom, we can imagine Henry obsessing over something Rev. Orestes Brownson had told him back during his tenure in Canton: "I am convinced," Brownson had said before Henry had yet formally taken charge of his first Canton class, "that a man who is fit to teach a school will never have occasion to strike a child."

This recollection of Brownson's words may have vindicated him and helped him settle his nerves. He *knew* he was fit to teach and knew too that inflicting pain and punishment was not the way to ensure learning happened. Time to move on. His days as a teacher in the Concord school system were over.

BUSINESS LESSON

It is only when we forget all our learning that we begin to know. Those moments when we are faced with challenges where solutions do not come easily are sometimes best managed by listening carefully to your gut. Forget the "rules" and "norms" that society dumps on us ending in a hemming-in rather than a clear path to the right decision. Heed your conscience, heed your instincts, trust your best judgment. In such confusing moments, prior "learning" is often little or no help.

Grab your favorite #2 and pencil in your business lesson here:

_____

_____

_____

4

HENRY INVENTS THE PENCIL . . . AS WE KNOW IT!

I know of no more encouraging fact
than the unquestionable ability of man
to elevate his life by conscious endeavor.

It had been gnawing at Henry, one can imagine, for most of the past week or two. He'd been fine for the few months or so that he'd agreed to return to his dad's little factory to help him out in return for room and board at home, his mother's boardinghouse where the Thoreau family now lived.

It seemed like a fair trade given the fact that Thoreau Pencils could always use his help just as he could use theirs, for mutual practical reasons. Plus Henry had literally been spending time alongside his dad in the pencil business off and on since a very young age.

The business started in 1821 when his uncle Charles Dunbar had been rummaging around the backwoods of southeastern New Hampshire seeking who-knows-what, and stumbled upon an undiscovered load of graphite, or plumbago as it used to be called, in the village of Bristol. Graphite/plumbago of course was the most essential ingredient for pencils, which suggested the gods of prosperity

had driven Dunbar to this very spot just so he could take advantage
of the find and upgrade his station in life.

The first phase of this new beginning, however, would be to set
up a mining operation that could extract this plumbago from the rich
New England soil and rock as a step toward using it to manufacture
pencils. Charles next wisely endeavored to get his find "certified" as
one of the best—if not *the* best—plumbago in all the United States.

Once experts who examined it did so certify, the world seemed
Charles Dunbar's oyster. Or at least things looked that way until legal
issues reduced his mine privileges to a mere seven-year lease. This
severely complicated matters, forcing Dunbar to pick up the pace of
extraction and somehow get actual pencils manufactured from his
plumbago ASAP.

But since Dunbar could obviously not manage all these operations by himself, he called upon—ta-da!—Henry's dad, John Thoreau
Sr. Then, for reasons no one seems to have ever recorded, Dunbar
had to drop out of the business entirely, leaving John on his own
to develop this new company, which he felt entitled to name John
Thoreau & Company.

So now the prosperity gods seemed to have crowned John rather
than Charles as worthy of their favors such that *this time*, despite
all his stabs at success in prior jobs and careers and businesses,
Henry's dad met with great success. By 1824, when Henry was only
seven, Thoreau Pencils had already acquired a reputation of such
lofty esteem that an exhibition of the Massachusetts Agricultural
Society deemed Thoreau "lead pencils" on exhibit at the fair as the
best in all the land. And in the years following, such success would
continue, rising steadily throughout Henry's childhood right up until
the time he headed for Harvard. By then, Henry had become quite
familiar with and appreciative of his family's famous business and all
it was known for.

But now, years later, though a graduate of Harvard yet somewhat
unsure how to restart his teaching career, Henry needed to pay his
mom some rent. Joining the intimate crew at Thoreau Pencils offered
one kind of solution, at least for the time being.

Though, in many ways, Henry's new gig was a mindless job of lifting heavy bags of plumbago and hauling cords of pencil wood, the daily grind of churning out much-needed pencils to replace the centuries-old writing tool kit of quill and inkwell did, nonetheless, present a few intriguing intellectual challenges. For one thing, even the best pencils produced in the United States, including Thoreau Pencils, came out as finished products that were frequently, in part or whole, greasy, gooey, gritty, brittle, liquid, impossible to stay stuck to paper, fragile, and therefore inefficient.

This meant that even Thoreau Pencils, though accepted by many as among *the* finest, of any similar product in all the United States, even their quality, in terms of consistency, proved not much better than the consistency of Thoreau's competitors. Top-of-the-line pencils in those days bore little resemblance to the caliber of pencils we take for granted today with all their predictable legibility, clarity, ease of reading, neatness, and, above all, reliability to write or sketch excellently well . . . first time, every time!

We can imagine that Henry immediately could see these problems when he rejoined the firm. And the more he saw, the more he could not dismiss them, surely telling himself there must be a better way, shaking his head as he likely thought to himself, *Why do we assume that this is the way pencils have to be?*

John Sr., who by now knew (and trusted) that Henry was developing solutions to his bafflement, probably responded to his son's frustrations with, "Yes, Henry, you're right. We'll send you back to Harvard and have you attempt to discover a better way." Easily convinced that if anyone could return from a week or two of research with practical plans in hand for advancing a solution to a problem such as this one, it would be Henry, he may have added, "Take a few days, take a week or two. Let's see what you can find back at the Harvard library. How else will we know?"

Shortly thereafter, Henry hopped aboard a stagecoach for Cambridge with his travel bag in tow, venturing eastward to learn what he could learn. Henry invariably preferred walking—even thirty-five-mile treks to Wachusett Mountain or day-long rambles to Flints Pond in Lincoln. But those excursions were for fun and recreational exploration; *this* would be a *business* trip. His objective: study, research, and scientific analysis that might answer these pressing questions:

- What methods might Henry discover for dramatically improving the family's products?
- How were other practitioners doing things differently?
- What differing methods were actually improving their manufacture of pencils?
- What did the United States' leading thinkers have to say about potential solutions?
- The bottom line? No time to waste!

Two hours later, Henry skipped out of the coach and stepped carefully onto the cobblestones of Massachusetts Avenue that he had become so familiar with in his student years at Harvard. Allowing the bustle of students, professors, and day-workers to brush past him before crossing the street to Harvard Yard, he passed through the main gate and sauntered across the green to the main library building where he would set up camp every day until he found what he had come searching for.

As with all research, the beginning moved slowly. Questions were legion:

- What books should he ask for?
- Whose idea was the first pencil, and when and where?
- Who now criticizes the accepted process and why?
- Who might be a pioneering expert in the field of pencil-making?
- Were there any trends in the industry, novel ideas, predictions for the future?

- How had pencil-making evolved over time?
- What can be done about pencils' failings in a consistent manner that replaces them with truly successful practices?

Over the course of often long days spent at Harvard's library, hints to the answers began to break through, like the tiny buds on the underbrush Henry knew so intimately along the shore of Walden Pond in early spring. Finally, however, the dawn itself began to break. Starting with discoveries of methods *outside* the United States, in Germany to be precise, with some spreading to France, experiments built their way into facts, facts into revelations, revelations giving birth to potential solutions. The key, Henry detected, seemed to lie especially within the best "recipe" for a pencil's interior, that is, the writing material itself.

Clay Mixed with Graphite

In the 1840s, European countries might as well have been as distant as Mars or Venus. With the telegraph still in its infancy, and trains and telephones not yet commonplace, books and letters remained the bridge between minds across continents.

But fortunately to an avid reader like Henry, books typically did the trick. With sufficient time, effort, and attention, this was a process that Henry was especially good at—nay, *great* at. Consequently, before long, he had identified not only a new recipe to replace the conventional standby but also a "contraption" to mix the ingredients in a way similar to what European pencil-makers had been utilizing for years with great success. In that regard, Henry improved upon not only the American way but the successful European way as well.

"The inferiority of American pencils was due in large part to the fact that pure English graphite—the world's best—was not readily available, and knowledge of a new European process for making pencils had apparently not yet reached [American] shores," wrote Henry Petroski, professor of civil engineering and history at Duke

University and author of *The Pencil: A History of Design and Circumstance.*

In an article for *Invention & Technology Magazine*, Petroski explained: "The French inventor Nicolas-Jacques Conté had discovered in the mid-1790s that clay mixed with graphite and then baked into a ceramic rod made far better pencil leads than graphite alone or combined with other substances; this innovation is the basis of all modern pencil making."

Firms like John Thoreau's, however, out of ignorance, had no reason to question their own pencil mixtures, laden as they were with "inadequately purified and graphite ground with such substances as glue, bayberry wax, and spermaceti (a waxy solid obtained from the oil of the sperm whale). The warmed mixture was pressed into a paste and poured or applied with a brush to the grooved part of a cedar case, and another piece of cedar was glued on top."

Henry knew that Thoreau graphite was of excellent quality and he deduced that the problem must have lain with the filler or in the lead-making process itself. He then proceeded to integrate clay but with unacceptable results due to Henry's pencil mixture still coming out too gritty. This led him next to wonder if the solution lay not in the recipe but the grinding process, the need to produce graphite finer than anyone else thought necessary.

Here's Henry Petroski again: "It is unclear exactly how much Henry and his father interacted in developing a new grinding mill for graphite, which was the next step, but Henry apparently worked out all the mechanical details, such as how fine to grind the graphite and how to remove the impurities that made pencil leads scratch."

Petroski then cites Edward Emerson, Waldo's son, as suggesting that the solution consisted in designing a "narrow churn-like chamber around the millstones prolonged some seven feet high, opening into a broad, close, flat box, a sort of shelf. Only lead-dust that was fine enough to rise to that height, carried by an upward draught of air and then lodge in the box was used. The rest was ground over."

Walter Harding, for many years perhaps *the* principal biographer of Henry, as if picking up the ball, further described what happened next: "The machine spun around inside a box set on a table and could be wound up to run itself so it could easily be operated by Henry's sisters."

By varying the amount of clay in the mixture, Thoreau Pencils could now produce pencils of different hardness and blackness, just as the European pencil-makers had once discovered. Simply put, the more plumbago a pencil lead contained, the harder would be the point, and the finer the grade of the chosen clay/plumbago, the more reliable and consistent it would be throughout its lifetime.

The result? Thanks to Henry's breakthrough, business at Thoreau Pencils began to soar. The demand was so strong that the introduction of this "refined graphite" spurred an expansion so great that John Thoreau decided to restrict access to the premises by the general populace because he did not want to spend money patenting their machines nor risk revealing their secret formula.

By 1844 Thoreau Pencils were easily superior to any available in the United States, whether domestic or foreign. Waldo, excitedly impressed with this new version, sent a bundle of pencils to a friend in Boston, and in that way, word began to get around that there was a new pencil "sheriff" in town, and nothing in the realm of writing tools would ever be the same again. Henry had basically reinvented the pencil as we know it.

Thoreau Pencils Transformed

In its new business incarnation, Thoreau Pencils quickly rose to the top of the heap in the US pencil trade, turning out a product that performed neatly every time. No more messy blotches on paper, no more liquid lead on fingers and desks, only clear, usable writing utensils that no one had to worry about before beginning to write or draw.

As well, pencils could now be customized as tools for a variety of professional specialties given the flexibility of the refinement process so that pencil numbers and levels of softness and hardness—the system we are accustomed to today—can be manufactured to meet the demands of the marketplace as needed. Almost two hundred years later, the standard is now the #2 pencil for general use—*all* of us!—while a more complicated system serves the needs of specific professionals such as artists and architects.

For architectural drawing alone, for example, the current range of pencil grades employed include H ("hardness") pencils (2H, 3H, etc.) capable of precise lines and outlines, and B ("blackness") soft pencils (2B, 4B, 6B, etc.) for shading and darkness. Landscapers also have their own recommendations.

What hath Henry wrought!

Additionally, there would also come a day when Henry would succeed his father in the role of owner and chief executive of the pencil factory following John Sr.'s death in 1859. As the only logical successor, Henry took the reins and held them for several years, managing it and leading in such a way that the company grew and prospered. One of his first acts of leadership was to acquire a copy of *Businessman's Assistant*, a guidebook aimed at teaching entrepreneurs to navigate the legal aspects of their operations. A collection of essential legal forms, leases, and contracts for business transactions was included in the book for convenience.

Once stable, the Thoreau Pencils enterprise was transformed even more drastically from a simple seller of pencils to, more and more, a wholesaler of ground plumbago. The first such potential buyer of its superior graphite, a Boston printing firm, confessed that Thoreau plumbago was ideal for a newly invented printing process called electrotyping, and for that reason, the ground plumbago was deemed more important than the pencils themselves and made available in the US, the UK, Europe, etc.

Thus, Henry could eventually move on from pencil manufacturing by delegating day-to-day operations to others, in particular his sister Sophia, who was adept at paperwork, an area where Henry was *not*! He could thus return to his true loves: writing, exploring, nature, philosophizing. But friends and family wondered why he had chosen to not continue minding the shop himself and keep turning out pencils.

In true Henry style, he put a lid on this questioning of his life choices by retorting: *Why should I? I would not do again what I have done once.*

Spoken like a true entrepreneur! On to other big things and adventures!

NOTE FROM YOUR AUTHOR

Henry once said he had "faith in a seed," and with that nugget in mind, I'll reveal that the tiny seed that led to this book was planted in my brain by Jeff Cramer, author of *The Portable Thoreau*, who at that time was curator of Collections at the Walden Woods Project's Thoreau Institute Library. I had met Jeff at his office where I had come to pick up an item I had successfully bid for in the annual Thoreau Society/Thoreau Farm auction.

While there, Jeff showed me a wall display containing a glassed-in showcase of a pencil from the mid-nineteenth century. "That pencil," Jeff informed me, "was created by Henry Thoreau. Without it we might never have known the standard reliable pencil we take for granted today." Then he told me all about how that happened just as I have done for you in this chapter.

I was amazed! I had never heard that Henry invented the pencil as we now know it. This fact stuck with me for many months, then silently, steadily grew into the flower of this book. If not for that visit, this book would likely never have happened.

Thanks, Jeff!

BUSINESS LESSON

It is not enough to be industrious; so are the ants. What are you industrious about? At times what works best is to take a step or two back, breathe deeply, count to ten or maybe twenty, peer up at the sky and clouds . . . then decide what first step to take, take it, and move carefully from there one step at a time. You'll be moving in a direction where you know what you are busy about as opposed to merely busy.

Grab your favorite #2 and pencil in your business lesson here:

_____

_____

_____

5

HENRY DAVID THOREAU, ENTREPRENEUR

Only he is successful in his business who makes that pursuit which affords him the highest pleasure to sustain him.

After the debacle of quitting his Concord teaching position, Henry resumed his job search, reaching out to contacts far and wide. He turned first to his brother, John, a teacher in West Roxbury, and his sister Helen, also a teacher in a school district many miles from Concord, but the economic turmoil of the Panic of 1837 had frozen education hiring statewide. Even these strong ties yielded no promising opportunities.

Driven by mounting desperation, Henry ventured to Maine, but nothing came of it. Returning to Concord empty-handed after a few weeks away, he rejoined Thoreau Pencils. There, as we've seen, he would one day channel his frustrations into innovation—revolutionizing pencil manufacturing in ways that have endured for generations.

But first, suddenly, he had a bright idea! Why not start his own school? What better business to start than a school! Surveying the educational offerings in Concord, he came to realize that Concord's official public school system was lacking—he had certainly found that out the hard way! Maybe a gap could be filled by operating a school in the way that *he* thought best.

Managing to locate a small meeting space in the heart of Concord village, Henry began spreading the word that his would be a very progressive school unlike any that had come before. There'd be instruction, yes; the three *R*'s, too; and studying the classics, of course, but adding conversational dialogues and moving them more to center stage rather than rote memorization. This would be the prevailing standard of *his* classroom days. Plus time would be spent outside the walls of Henry's classroom, especially on special days (often a Saturday afternoon) when a nature walk with Henry might bring his small initial group of local youngsters to such perfect learning spots as Walden Pond and additionally to other mystical locales with names like Great Meadows, Haywood Meadow, and Sandy Pond.

On these outings, Henry's "assignments" included exotic searches for Indian arrowheads—often right below one's feet if they only crouched down to dig with their fingers in the dirt (Henry was spectacular at this!)—canoeing around a pond or down one of Concord's rivers, or sauntering through Walden Woods. All the while, he wove Socratic dialogues connecting wilderness and the human spirit to transcendentalism's three core beliefs: individualism, idealism, and the divinity of nature.

During such field trips, Henry's academy students likely occasionally caught a glimpse of one or more prominent transcendentalist pioneers, such as Waldo, Bronson Alcott, Ellery Channing, Margaret Fuller, or Elizabeth Palmer Peabody. They too embarked daily to Walden's paths and meadows or to the infinite bustle of the center of Concord commerce, what the locals labeled the Milldam.

With the aid of prominent, affluent Concordian fathers—Samuel Hoar, John Keyes, and Nathan Brooks, among others—Henry's first school season welcomed four paying students, then slowly but steadily watched its numbers grow. The task falling to Henry then was to do it all: instruct, counsel, motivate, and enroll. The first year, it grew to only ten or so students, but eventually many more.

This drew the attention of his brother, John, who also had been feeling hemmed in by the requirements of employment at a conventional school, similar to those in Concord. Before long, John resigned his position to move back to Concord and partner with his brother in a takeover of Concord Academy, now in dire straits, that the Thoreau kids themselves had attended back in their early years.

From "Employee" to "Entrepreneur"

In addition to the unique curriculum the brothers introduced, there would of course be *no* corporal punishment allowed. This was a feature that onlookers in Concord couldn't believe. One Concordian swore he had no idea how they achieved such a positive, orderly learning environment that put the usual standard—flogging—out to pasture. But succeed they did, generating a level of trust and appreciation in the students and creating a supportive atmosphere within their school and outside it in the village as well. This would be especially remembered by their young protégés for as long as they lived.

The revitalized "Concord Academy" enhanced Henry's reputation in Concord, bestowing upon him the honor of being treated as a refreshing new "pillar of the community." More important for Henry's personal development, his new venture swayed his mind from identifying as an *employee* or *job-holder* to more self-affirming labels like *entrepreneur*, *founder*, and *business owner*. But there were both pros and cons to this change:

1. CON: No guaranteed salary or steady paycheck!
An entrepreneur's income is based entirely on successfully attracting "customers" every year. Rather than landing that *one* big customer typically referred to as one's employer, Henry needed to keep up the flow of customers and revenue nonstop, or his employment would end.

2. PRO: No single "boss" to report to, except for one's customers.
Instead of a supervisor to watch over Henry and tell him what to do, including making up arbitrary rules, the entrepreneur's "boss" is typically the customer base or target market. Although a board of directors might be added as a check and balance or to serve in an advisory role, the bottom line was to please customers and keep the revenue flowing while spreading positive word of mouth in the form of prospect referrals and endorsements from satisfied customers.

3. PRO: The good news in #2 is that no one individual (i.e., one's boss) can summarily fire the entrepreneur.
Instead the entrepreneurs may fire those who work under and for them!

4. CON: The bad news in #2 is that the entrepreneur is responsible for seeing that everything is always functioning properly and excellently.
Ongoing sales must be made and the company overall must, in turn, keep churning out its product or service with maximum efficiency and quality.

5. CON: Headaches often come home with the entrepreneur at the end of the day.
Company bills to pay, customers' orders to fulfill, customer complaints all must be addressed. In contrast, employees may punch out and head home without carrying the load of their workday with them. Or at least that was true back in Henry's day, long before our current 24/7 online era!

6. PRO: The focus of the work derives from YOU!
Last but by no means least, starting one's own business enables the founder to determine exactly what the focus of work within the company's walls will be, not only for the founder but also for the founder's executive team and workforce and even customers. Henry had

always been concerned about the issue of working throughout one's lifetime only for the sake of paying bills versus enjoying a large part of his day or feeling fulfilled by the work itself. Was this "making a living" approach equal to "making a life," he used to remark and write in his journal. Assuming the role of entrepreneur supports this.

Writing in *Medium*, blogger Oshan Jarow, a consciousness studies and political economy thoughtleader, analyzed the dichotomy in his 2018 post "Making a Living as Making a Life: Thoreau on Work & Life's Real Business" this way:

"We work so much just to survive that in the process we forfeit ourselves to the cyclical process of securing *means*, leaving far too little time for the exploration of *ends*." He then quotes Henry's thinking regarding the whole world as a *"place of business"* and an *"infinite bustle!"* followed by this declaration from Henry: *I think that there is nothing, not even crime, more opposed to poetry, to philosophy, ay, to life itself, than this incessant business.*

"Why? Is work, all work, so holy?" Jarow asks. "Is a future replete with work really the best we can envision? What of kindness, wisdom, stability, or happiness, to name a few? Such a work-centric future would horrify Thoreau, who laments the unconscious, thoughtless conflation between making a living—work—and living itself."

> It is remarkable that there is little or nothing to be remembered written on the subject of getting a living; how to make getting a living not merely holiest and honorable, but altogether inviting and glorious; for if getting a living is not so, then living is not.

Jarow writes, "Thoreau continues, pointing at the inadequacy of responding to philosophy's question with the near-sightedness of merely economic considerations . . ."

> The ways in which most men get their living, that is, live, are mere makeshifts, and a shirking of the real business of

life—chiefly because they do not know, but partly because they do not mean, any better.

Later Jarow adds that if Henry "still hits the mark that our means of making a living actually shirk *the real business of life*'—we may be left feeling slightly defensive, uncomfortable with our implicated accountability. But perhaps we can still dodge the blame." Here's Henry again, one more time:

If we have thus desecrated ourselves—as who has not?—the remedy will be by wariness and devotion to reconsecrate ourselves, and make once more a fane [shrine] of the mind.

And finally Jarow again, following up to help us bridge any gap we may still have with Henry's thinking: "That society encourages the growth of individuals, each his own shrine, is Thoreau's vision. Work should not keep us too busy for ourselves, but nudge us evermore towards ourselves. That our laborious activity—how we make a living—should not thicken but distill the opaque film of selfhood, revealing evermore universal intuitions."

Unlike at the public school where the brothers had previously taught, where except for an hour of "recess" students spent their day memorizing, reading, and listening to lectures, all of it indoors, all of it seated and well-behaved (or else!), the school day at the Concord Academy consisted of two segments: first, time *inside* the classroom for attention to the classics, mathematics, history, and so forth. Then second, *outside* the classroom where air and energy and discovery and wonder roamed as free as the birds fluttering overhead and the small critters scampering in and out of thickets.

Would such a combination brew a shrine of the mind? Would it allow Henry's protégés to breathe in and out, to imagine, attempt, and enjoy, thence ultimately choose *for themselves* the best-fit "work" direction in which they might go as they transformed into integral toilers in society? Henry was banking that the answer to both questions would be yes.

Should Tragedy Strike

With all these pros and cons, considerations, and requisites in play, should tragedy strike, whether economic recession or something more personal, the decision for how to handle such a challenge was entirely up to the entrepreneur. This too came with the territory.

So when suddenly, horribly, John contracted tetanus, possibly from a rusty blade while shaving, Henry stayed by his bedside for three days in agony, worried that John would not survive which, sadly, is exactly what happened. To Henry, John's passing was devastating.

As a result, heartbroken and adrift without his brother, Henry shuttered the Concord Academy. John had been the glue holding their venture together, and his absence was now an unfillable void. After losing John, Henry could not imagine continuing alone.

As time passed, however, one can imagine that Henry slowly began to have a realization: *His* ideas for running the school had made this enterprise a success, validating his instincts and buoying his sense of himself and of what he would be able to accomplish in his life.

The reality of this insight, that his own ideas translated into a business venture could be a winner, stuck with Henry for the rest of his life. Even when he later signed on with Waldo to serve as personal handyman at Bush, Emerson's modest estate, he could now do so with an inner knowledge that this new gig was just that: a gig. It would not become his life's work; it was not to be a "career." Even in such employment arrangements, he would likely think of himself as an independent practitioner (or contractor, as we say today) whether teaching or tutoring children, land surveying a farm or town boundary, or helping out at Thoreau Pencils.

Yet it must also be considered as well that the truest entrepreneur is a creative, idea-crazy, risk-taking soul living life through in the same spirit and mindset as the truest artist. Art, contrary to conventional wisdom, does not mean greatness or obvious talent every time out of the box. Art sometimes succeeds while other times it fails, even miserably.

How else to explain why a motion picture with a cast and crew and director of great renown will sometimes fail at the box office, despite the usual onslaught of millions of dollars in advertisements, appearances by the film's director and leading actors on the talk shows and podcasts, plus gigantic billboards in Times Square plus other types of promotion?

Why does a new book from a best-selling novelist sometimes fall flat with both reviewers and the author's reading public despite their talent and devoted followers?

Why do singers and musicians express frustration when rabid fans pony up hundreds of dollars per ticket but on the concert tour seem uninterested in the performers' "new stuff," screaming loudly for hit songs from decades ago?

All this is to say that entrepreneurs, same as artists, sometimes fail. Risk-taking ensures this, since sometimes risk will pay off and other times it will not. But nothing will happen if a risky idea isn't at least *tried*, or acted upon. Back in my earlier days as a career coach, I had a mantra about this for my clients exploring a career change that went, "Failure is desirable." That was because, as conventional sales wisdom goes, if you fail at selling your services or product to a prospect, then your next move has to be to try to sell to a *new* prospect. If that fails as well, have no fear because sooner or later, maybe as many as twenty failed attempts in a row, you *will* ultimately sell to someone! Then if you keep on keeping track of your failure-to-sell ratio and, as an example, discover that it takes you nineteen failures to reach that one-in-twenty success, you have now defined how many failures you need to endure to achieve a success. From then on, you can be confident that each failed attempt will bring you closer and closer to landing a new customer or client. Thus failure, within such context, is *desirable*!

Henry apparently felt the same. In a *National Geographic* article, "Bitter Berries: The Historic Battle for Cranberry Power Bars," Rebecca Rupp recounts the frustrating 1849 saga of Henry's "brief financial flutter" with cranberries: "Hard put to pay for his cellar full of unsold copies of his first book, Thoreau came up with a scheme to work off his debt by selling cranberries to New York City. First he priced berries in Boston's Quincy Market, with an eye to purchasing an 'indefinite quantity' which 'made a slight sensation,' he later wrote in his journal, 'and for aught I know raised the price of the berry for a time.'

"He then checked out freight costs on ships bound for New York (on deck or in the hold), and found a cooperative skipper 'very anxious' to take on a cargo of cranberries. As a final step, he checked out the selling price of cranberries in New York and found, to his dismay, that they were markedly cheaper there than in Boston. The deflated Thoreau finally paid off his $100 debt by selling pencils from the family pencil factory (instead)."

Should Henry have never even started down this road to a cranberry venture that he hoped would answer all his debt struggles? Easy to say today, well after the fact. But as a genuine entrepreneur, he couldn't stop himself from seeing what might result. Little could he imagine that his bright idea would be a bust. But the long and short of it is that sometimes entrepreneurs just plain strike out—no other comforting way to frame it.

Laura Dassow Walls adds: "Well, I think the cranberry venture was doomed from the start, but hey, he learned something even from that failure! In fact, I think this is true of his other less-than-successful 'career' attempts: Editing *The Dial* with Emerson was a frustrating time-suck, but he learned from it, both about precision in editing and that editing was not the best use of his skill set. He learned too from a failed tutoring job on Staten Island that he wasn't good at working with dull students."

He *learned* something. That is just what entrepreneurs do.

HENRY FACTS

Much, much later a private prep school by the same name as the one the Thoreau brothers founded, i.e., The Concord

Academy (TCA), would be founded in 1922. No relationship at all to the earlier TCA and still in operation in Concord today.

BUSINESS LESSON

Do not hire a man who works only for money but him who does his work for the love of it. When founding a business, envision how you want it to be, not how others have done it. Your way will be the right way for you and for those who choose to follow you by actually *paying* for your product or service!

Grab your favorite #2 and pencil in your business lesson here:

_____

_____

_____

6

MASTER BUILDER

If a man does not keep pace with his companions,
perhaps it is because he hears a different drummer.
Let him step to the music which he hears.

A manifestation of writing, exploring, and philosophizing revealed itself in Henry's 1845 decision to build himself a cabin in the woods located a few dozen footsteps from the shore of Walden Pond. He articulated his main motivation in *Walden*, inspiring millions of Thoreauvians in the two centuries since its publication. Here's how he expressed it in *Walden*:

> *I went to the woods because I wished to live deliberately, to*
> *front only the essential facts of life, and see if I could not learn*
> *what it had to teach, and not, when I came to die, discover that*
> *I had not lived.*

Based on the eventual behavior that Henry exhibited during his time at the pond, it seems, though, that his motivation was for a quieter and calmer environment more conducive to writing than the often noisy boardinghouse where he grew up.

But in the beginning, writing was not a high priority for Henry at Walden Pond due to his need to set up his living and working conditions so that he could later turn to writing as his focus. So in the beginning, he attended more to business and working lines of thought than to more passionate and "dream career" endeavors.

His design of the cabin, for example, spawned a precise accounting of every single penny of its costs. And his ability to fit all the little building's pieces together, typically solely on his own, demonstrated a business brain like no other.

One exception was the roof-raising, wherein he enlisted the help of friends and family so as to get the job done in less than a day. But as for materials and tools needed, he did whatever he could to keep costs as low as possible, such as, for instance, borrowing an axe from a friend rather than purchasing one and maintaining the dimensions of his cabin to such a minimum that he traded the capacity to entertain visitors and maybe throw the occasional party (!) for a solace that most of us might find too ascetic to accept. He often remarked, somewhat proudly it seemed, that the size of his abode (as we noted earlier) allowed for only *three chairs in my house: one for solitude, two for friendship, three for society.*

Thus, upon completing his ever-so-humble, no-place-like-home personal palace, he simultaneously completed a now-famous painstaking list of his actual construction costs, faithful down to every last farthing. Here's the original, impeccable list with Henry's original spelling and grammar intact:

- Board's: $8.03½ , mostly shanty boards
- Refuse shingles for roof and sides: $4.00
- Laths: $1.25
- Two second-hand windows with glass: $2.43
- One thousand old brick: $4.00
- Two casts of lime: $2.40. That was high.
- Hair: $0.31. More than I needed
- Mantle-tree iron: $0.15
- Nails: $3.90

- Hinges and screws: $0.14
- Latch: $0.10
- Chalk: $0.01
- Transportation: $1.40. I carried a good part on my back.
- In all: $28.12½

To this no-frills accounting, Henry ends with this notation: *"These are all the materials excepting the timber, stones, and sand, which I claimed by squatter's right."*

Henry was therefore able to erect his cabin on a little rise about fifty steps from the lapping shore of Concord's favorite pond in a small curved-shore area that would come to be known as Henry's Cove. With his front (and only) door positioned so that it faced the water to the east, he could wake up to the New England sunrise that caused the pond to sparkle with a morning delight. Stretching outside his cabin as he yawned and shook himself awake, he would typically saunter down to the water's edge, dip a toe in the chilly pool, then wade slowly ahead until deep enough to plunge forward into his morning swim.

He claimed to do this every morning except in the winter months when the ice was stiff. Then he would have pivoted to a different morning routine, likely snowshoeing through an overnight drop of snow or skating across Walden Pond.

But what better way to wake up? He must have brought to mind this rhetorical question a million times. On swim mornings Walden would envelop and embrace him, wrapping its misty cloak all around him while crying out to him that he was "home," that is, where he ought to be. A partnership such as this made all things right.

After his swim, according to his journal entries, he would have his usual breakfast of grains, beans, and vegetables while sitting by his fireplace or out on a fallen log, surrounded by the critters who called this forest their home before Henry's cabin was even conceived. His most frequent dining companion was an amiable mouse who, over days of patient courtship, progressed from merely approaching to quickly grabbing morsels from Henry's open hand before scooting away. A squirrel or skittish chipmunk might do the same, while a nuthatch—just as tentative—would peck at scraps tossed from Henry's plate or frying pan outside the cabin door.

Following breakfast, Henry settled in to work for a bit, which for him meant writing a letter or poem or a few pages for his new book. This took place at his green wooden writing desk (acquired from his brother, John) followed by a few hours' excursion out and about the pond's woods. The agenda for these excursions read the same every day: Observe nature, keep eyes open for arrowheads below and bald eagles above, saunter to wherever his inquisitive self would direct him, and frequently chat up "pond folk" who either lived at Walden as squatters as he did or deeper within the woods, perhaps ex-slaves or poor farmhands.

One friendly group he could always count on were the Boston-to-Fitchburg railroad workers come to lay track by the far shore of Walden or repair railroad ties or clear brush and tree branches so the trains could come through. Henry's fascination with the railroad at that point, however, was conflicted. First, he was unsure if such technology was even warranted. Why cart so many Concordians off to work in the big city when they might stay right here in Concord and serve Concordians? Second, an opposite thought, why bring Bostonians *into* Concord to sweat away in the Damon Mill textile factory when so many such sweatshops could just as easily be found back in the city?

Yet, although there were reasons to doubt the railroad's value, there was also a positive benefit to it that he came more and more to appreciate. It certainly made life easier and more comfortable for someone like him who loved to trek into Boston on any given day, browse for hours in a library or bookstore or museum at Harvard, then saunter around the streets of Boston to see what he might see along its wharf or on a hill in its public common, or while looking up toward the top of some newly built brick "skyscraper" . . . six stories high!

After marveling at all this, Henry need only hop back on a train heading west and be comfortably back in Concord within the hour, skipping the roughness of a coach completely. Over time, the long, cramped, dusty stagecoach rides were rendered to a thing of the past.

Yes, the railroad was something to behold and appreciate once you got to know them!

Networking Around the Pond . . .

"Hail there! How goes your work today?" Henry must have uttered often. Such greetings would invariably pause the work of anyone toiling out of doors during even the coldest months of the year—even ice-cutters working at Walden Pond in an area still known today as Ice Fort Cove. These greetings must have gotten the men's attention, eliciting a friendly wave and perhaps a chat as they found themselves drawn into conversation by Henry's curiosity.

One imagines that his questions would focus on ice cutting as well as successful building techniques, as many ice cutters would likely spend warmer months building or repairing domiciles of all types and sizes. Such experience afforded them practical wisdom: how to re-shingle a roof or alleviate pressure from heavy snowfalls or, in warmer seasons, keep torrential rains from causing leaks. To Henry, this level of momentary mentorship must have felt worth its weight in gold. Real-world experiences like these he never picked up at Harvard.

Happening upon a squatter or owner of a shack within Walden's environs would have similarly elicited golden advice. "What do you do to keep your house warm in winter?" he may have asked a "neighbor."

"Well, I try to pile on beech kindling," the neighbor might respond. "I keep it handy for when I wake up at night and it's too cold for sleeping. So I throw on some more kindling with a new log and crawl back into bed, toasty-like."

Networking—ambling around and striking up conversations with whomever—proved useful to Henry as he became a master at building. For him, learning from others was an enjoyable lifelong behavior, and he never shied away from chance meetings. Every conversation planted seeds of knowledge, and networking of this sort always struck him as natural as a walk in the forest on a bright, sunny day.

This would also serve him well in situations away from the pond, such as when Bronson Alcott, Louisa May's father, asked him for help installing an addition to the Orchard House, the family homestead, situated just a half mile from Bush, Waldo's home. And such advice from his networking would have also enhanced Henry's ability to repair the loft in Waldo's barn or perhaps expand a room in Waldo's house or build a shed to store tools and paint cans. As Waldo had no clue how to perform any of these tasks, he counted on his young friend, not only to help him build or repair things but also to share his ideas and expertise in such matters and be quick with practical suggestions and the occasional novel idea.

In addition, Henry had learned a fair amount about building in 1844, the year *before* he built his cabin at Walden Pond, after spending much of that year expanding his knowledge of construction while building a house from scratch with his father for the family to move into. The neighborhood is now a very busy area of Concord thanks to its train depot, the town's first rail stop.

Back then, however, this section of town had only just begun to get rail service, partially because train travel was so new and also because the area was so far from Concord proper that it might as well have been in Texas! Thus this new Thoreau home came to be known as the Texas House and later the street was also so-named after what would become a year later our twenty-eighth state. For Henry, though, who loved to walk, it was a perfect location for sauntering to and from his cabin, day or night, or up to the village, located not very far away to his way of thinking versus many villagers' perceptions that a ten-minute walk was too far away!

Calculating Henry's Profit-Loss at Walden

Business is all about profit, so to be genuinely deemed a success, an individual, team, or organization must be able to translate their activities into positive ROI—a profitable return on investment. In that regard, no less a "Henry-watcher" than Walter Harding, generally acclaimed to be Henry's foremost biographer, once declared that Henry's time spent at Walden was indeed "a complete success" if relating its evaluation as a business. But how did Harding determine this judgment?

Because details are sketchy in that aspect of Harding's work, it has fallen upon others to test the details of Henry's "experiment" in order to confirm (or dispute) Harding's assessment. Among these later evaluators, the most prominent to emerge has been economist Thomas J. Miceli, professor of economics at the University of Connecticut and a longtime member of the Thoreau Society. In an essay in the spring 2005 *Thoreau Society Bulletin*, Miceli took up the challenge of analyzing all the facts at hand and pronouncing a verdict.

So beginning with Henry's detailed accounting of his income and expenses in the opening chapter of *Walden*, Miceli reports: "According to his own calculations, [Henry] lost $25.21¾ during that year, which actually understated his loss since he did not account for the cost of the land on which he squatted. [Thus] his oversight suggests that his experiment may have been less than a success in economic terms."

Miceli then pivots to the recognition that "of course, turning a profit was not Thoreau's primary objective, but in view of the importance that he himself attached to the economic aspects of his venture"—after all, "Economy" is the first and longest chapter in the book, he points out—then "we are entitled to evaluate it on those grounds. A fair evaluation, however, requires use of the correct methodology; that is the purpose of my article."

The first step, then, in properly calculating Henry's *profitability* here is to "distinguish between his net operating income and the value of his fixed assets," he says, explaining: "Generally speaking, the net income (or profit) of a business enterprise is the amount by which the flow of income or revenue exceeds the expenses during a given period of time (a year, say). In contrast, the assets of a business consist of the fixed (durable) investments in land and capital (buildings) that can be used to produce a stream of income over a number of years."

Since the initial cost of these assets was a one-time expenditure, Miceli points out, it should not enter the calculation of profit but rather be employed as a basis for calculating the *rate* of profit earned by the enterprise. "Specifically, the ratio of the net income to the value of the assets (land plus capital) yields the rate of return on the assets. This return provides a measure of the efficiency of the enterprise, and hence it can be compared to the returns on alternative investments that the entrepreneur could have made. It also offers a meaningful basis for comparing the profitability of enterprises of different scales, which cannot be done with net income."

In view of the distinction between net income and asset value, Miceli continues, Henry's accounting of the profitability of his enterprise over the first year (which, as noted, showed a loss of $25.21¾) is therefore possibly deceptive as a measure of its true profitability on two counts, the first being the inclusion of a capital cost (his house) in his calculation of net income during the year, and second, Henry's ignoring the cost of the land altogether. "Thus, his calculations do not reveal the true profitability of his experiment," Miceli writes, adding:

> To do a proper calculation, we first need to determine Thoreau's net income, which consists of his gross income from the farm and from his non-farm labor:

Farm income	$23.44
Income from day labor	$13.34
TOTAL INCOME	**$36.78**

LESS HIS EXPENSES:

Farm one year	$14.72½
Food	$8.74
Clothing (eight months)	$8.40¾
Oil, etc. (eight months)	$2.00

TOTAL EXPENSES — **$33.87¼**

which yields:

$36.78
−$33.87¼

NET INCOME — **$2.90¾**

Miceli continues: "Next, we must consider the initial investment in capital. The cost of the house was $28.12½, which we will treat as the value of the capital. Ideally, we would like to know the market value of the house, which is what someone would have paid for it, but we have no evidence on what that amount would have been. In using construction cost, we are therefore probably understating the house's value, which will bias the rate of return upward."

Finally, Miceli turns our attention to the value of the land that Thoreau cultivated. Due to Waldo's special in-kind arrangement with Henry, where Waldo had agreed to waive rental fees in exchange for Henry's raising crops of beans and vegetables for consumption by Waldo's family, Henry's status was basically a squatter on the land rather than a renter. "But the land was not valueless," Miceli reminds us, and hence it would not be appropriate to treat it as a free input. Had Thoreau acquired the land from someone besides Emerson (or another like-minded patron), he would have had to pay the market rent.

"In effect, therefore, Emerson made a 'gift' of the rent to Thoreau by not charging him," Miceli continues. "Nevertheless, calculation of the true profitability of Thoreau's venture must account for the 'opportunity cost' of the land as reflected by its market value."

Henry also tells us that the eleven-acre parcel on which he squatted was sold for $8.08 an acre the previous year, generating a whole-parcel market value of $88.88. However, as he cultivated only two and a half acres of the parcel, the total value of the cultivated land was just $20.20. This, Miceli, says, combined with the value of the house, yields the total value of Henry's assets like this:

Value of house	$28.12½
Value of land	$20.20
TOTAL ASSET VALUE	**$48.32½**

Miceli then calculates that the ratio of Henry's net income to the total value of his assets yields this rate of return on assets:

$$\text{Return on assets} = \frac{(\$2.90\frac{3}{4})}{(\$48.32\frac{1}{2})} = 6.017\%$$

As a basis for comparison, Miceli presents a table (below) that displays the results of a comparable calculation for American farmers, at ten-year intervals, during the twentieth century (1910–2000). We see here that returns range from a low of 2.1% in 1980 to a high of 18.1% in 1950, with an average return of 9.6%. Thus, Henry's return, while somewhat below the average, is quite respectable, Miceli declares.

Return on Assets (Land and Buildings)
for American Farmers, 1910–2000

1910	12.0%
1920	11.7%
1930	8.9%
1940	13.3%
1950	18.1%
1960	9.2%
1970	8.1%
1980	2.1%
1990	7.7%
2000	4.8%

Despite these results, Miceli cautions that this comparison needs to be qualified in two significant ways.

First, as noted previously, Henry earned a substantial portion of his income (36.3%) from working as a surveyor, carpenter, and other forms of day labor. But if his income from farming alone were considered, he would have incurred a loss of $10.43¼ on the farm, yielding a negative return of 21.6%. Clearly, including his non-farm income "is crucial in reaching the conclusion that his overall experiment was profitable."

To be fair, Miceli also adds, "this is in keeping with American farmers who, in the twentieth century at least, had begun to earn a substantial portion of their income from non-farm sources." For example, US Department of Agriculture data indicates that the percent of farm operator income from non-farm sources grew dramatically in the late twentieth century, primarily due to increased use of labor-saving technologies in farming as well as to improved education levels of farm operators. "Both of these trends allowed (or necessitated) farmers to pursue other occupations while maintaining their farms."

Of course, in economic terms, this trend has greatly benefited farm families by partially insulating them from fluctuations in farm earnings due to weather and variable farm prices. Thus by practicing this form of income diversification, Henry had moved himself ahead of his contemporaries and to the forefront of this developing economic curve.

Miceli's second factor that needs to be considered to authenticate the level of profitability of Henry's experiment is what Miceli calls "the importance of (Henry's) non-pecuniary returns." In addition to a house and the monetary returns from selling his surplus crop, Henry notes a certain sense of secured "leisure and independence and health," which Miceli informs us are benefits that economists *do* include, alongside profit, as an important component of "the overall 'utility,' or level of satisfaction, that one receives from engaging in an activity or business." Consideration of these aspects is particularly relevant for the evaluation of the profitability of family farms (or any other family business, for that matter) wherein a business owner foregoes higher returns in other occupations "because of the perceived noneconomic benefits of farming as a way of life."

Ultimately, however, even beyond this X factor of "leisure and independence," it must also be considered that, during his time at Walden, Henry also produced two books, numerous lectures, "and countless journal entries that have been of incalculable value to subsequent generations of scholars, students, reformers, and admirers, not to mention the profits from sales of *Walden*." In this sense, Miceli summarizes, the rate of return calculated via the previous more conventional data "greatly understates the true 'profitability' of Thoreau's stay at Walden. All told, therefore, it is safe to conclude, that Henry's experiment was a 'complete success' after all."

Q&A WITH TOM MICELI, PROFESSOR OF ECONOMICS AT THE UNIVERSITY OF CONNECTICUT

What should people know about Henry in relation to work/career/ business that they do not know today?
I think the popular view of Thoreau today is that of a dilettante or a loafer, though his role as one of the founders of environmentalism is perhaps favorably superseding that image. Certainly, he is not seen as being associated with work or business. If anything, he is seen as anti-business, and there is some truth to that. But I think his industriousness is not known, probably because it strikes people as oxymoronic to say that someone who is anti-business is industrious. Again, it comes back to the difference in rewards one is pursuing by their industriousness.

What was Henry able to do well in a work-related area and/or accomplish that you envy?
I think his efforts at self-reliance at Walden Pond were what most attracted me to Henry in the first place. He was clearly a jack-of-all-trades when it came to getting along in life (perhaps not an

unusual thing in those days), which is what permitted him to succeed in his experiment. We, on the other hand, live in an age of specialization, which precludes even contemplating the sort of self-sufficiency that he achieved.

BUSINESS LESSON

Our life is frittered away by detail. Simplicity, simplicity, simplicity! Measure and keep records of everything you do. It pays to be meticulous and to run a business deliberately by tracking precisely where you have succeeded and how you might succeed even more. Having done all that, reduce your business to its simplest core. But don't cut corners! Quality should be Job One, so keep it there, no matter what.

Grab your favorite #2 and pencil in your business lesson here:

_____

_____

_____

7

MASTER FARMER

Why is the cellar so important? It holds root vegetables.

Part of the deal with Ralph Waldo Emerson, who lent Henry use of the patch of property he owned in Walden Woods, was for Henry, in lieu of rent, to raise string beans on a couple of acres of adjoining Emerson land that Waldo could then pass on to his wife, Lidian, for family dinners. But in carrying out this in-kind "rental" agreement, Henry exhibited such a knack for raising vegetables that he was also able to supply leftover beans to his mother for meals at the boardinghouse and to himself for his own meals at the cabin.

Some weeks he even had enough additional crops to offer them for sale in the center of town, at that time called the Milldam, and based on his own calculations, the resulting proceeds showed a profit that at times was greater than any of his local fellow farmers' yields.

In the previous chapter, we learned that, when his non-farm income was added to his farm income, Henry's time and effort spent at his Walden cabin could be deemed "profitable" and therefore a success. But what if *only* farm income was considered? How would Henry stack up against competing farmers in that case? What would an economist or historian have to say to that?

Monetizing His Bean Field

During his first year at Walden, Henry planted primarily string beans on approximately two acres of Waldo's garden land in addition to potatoes, turnips, and peas. He was known to have shun his boots in favor of grousing about up and down the vegetable rows in his bare feet plus taking breaks where, as we might imagine, he might first stare dreamily skyward, then level his gaze twenty feet in front of him at a stand of cedars, and finally turn his attention down a pathway toward the water sparkling atop Walden Pond itself. Yes, sure, he was functioning as a farmer now but likely appreciating his surroundings far more than most of his farming colleagues.

Of course, Henry also liked to let his instincts rule the day as well, and his anthropologic skillset, unearthing arrowheads and cracked ceramics stuck under the soil of his bean rows. Farming to him offered so much more than the tedium of hoeing and planting and weeding, what with the sublime air of all of nature 360 degrees around him. He was expert at transforming the standard brand of farming from a series of repetitive dusty, grimy chores into a very, very, very ongoing delight.

In terms of finances, Henry calculated in *Walden* that he tended to invest fifteen or so dollars on his crops in return for grossing twenty-four dollars, resulting in a profit of almost nine dollars. Not a bad haul in Henry's day! He also bartered a portion of his crop in exchange for rice from other farmers or merchants, potentially adding a few more additional dollars' profit, although how much, exactly, is impossible to calculate.

Yet more than that, Henry could never escape his astonishment at what he felt was the valuable role of the true farmer. Perhaps his main purpose in cultivating crops, he explains in *Walden*, was not so much to make a buck but to embrace transcendental experience. Nature was the point of it all, so whatever followed as a result—good or bad weather, or rich or poor soil, or coyotes, woodchucks, beavers doing what coyotes, woodchucks, beavers instinctively do, for good or ill to one's farm—was simply the way things were supposed to have gone.

Thus those "careful calculations" found in "Economy" fall by the wayside when Henry later reports that a hoe may have cost him fifty-four cents but that's okay because, in many ways, he confessed, he frequently struggled to understand why he was farming at all. Perhaps next season, he would choose to cease to sow beans at all and treat agriculture less as a source of healthy food but more as an indispensable gyrating needle on his moral compass, thus sowing another sort of indispensable seed, like, say, "sincerity, truth, simplicity, faith, and innocence."

Then, as if to balance his appreciation for farming with a fair warning about its downside to farmers, he cites their particular economic challenges that sometimes extend beyond their very reach, no matter how productive or resilient they attempt to be. Farmers, he admonishes, are faced day in and day out with "endeavoring to solve the problem of a livelihood by a formula more complicated than the problem itself," declaring solemnly, "To get his shoestrings, [a farmer must] speculate in herds of cattle." Planting and harvesting alone does not cut it.

We might say then that, although Henry appears to have proven that he did possess a certain profit-inducing skillset, at least a portion of that very skillset may be due not to having earned some CPA certification or an MBA degree but something altogether unexpected and unusual: a passionate love for the outdoors! Only this, Henry seems to be saying for farmers, only this will yield dependable and consistent profits by the end of each day or season.

Henry's Green Thumb

Beyond his actual farming on Waldo's land, Henry's de facto green thumb displayed itself in many other ways leading to non-monetary triumphs, but triumphs all the same.

The most enduring—and endearing!—of these was his planting of a vegetable garden as a wedding present to Nathaniel Hawthorne and his bride, Sophia, on July 9, 1842, on the grounds of a house they rented at the time called the Old Manse. Remarkably, the property's caretakers have faithfully replanted its garden every year since—a living tribute now approaching its third century. For all those thousands of tourists who have visited the Old Manse since the days when Henry organized and cultivated this vegetable garden, it typically elicits gasps when these tourists are told, or read in the accompanying plaque, that it has been replanted in the front yard of the Old Manse every year ever since its first day!

Henry's Reverence for Farmers

In addition to his own success in the limited amount of farming in which he engaged, Henry waxed frequently and eloquently about his admiration of farmers and their chosen profession. He had remarked in his journal, for example, that *successful farming admits of no idling . . . a farmer increases the extent of habitable earth. He makes soil. That is an honorable occupation.* He even compared, favorably, the farmer's lot with his own activities in his more scholarly profession, writing: *The scholar's and the farmer's work are strictly analogous. He is doing like myself. My barnyard is my journal.*

In *Walden*, he expresses his admiration for all the *fishermen, hunters, woodchoppers, and others, spending their lives in the fields and woods, often in a more favorable mood for observing nature, in the intervals of their pursuits, than philosophers or poets even, who approach her with expectation.* Interestingly, he doesn't include farmers specifically in this remark but, given his many positive notations of farmers in other sources, it's easy to assume that excluding them was just an oversight.

Henry tried his best to always pay attention to natural surroundings, including farming, that he felt many of these other lucky "outside workers" sometimes missed. Elsewhere in *Walden* he reports:

When my hoe tinkled against the stones, that music echoed to
the woods and the sky, and was an accompaniment to my labor
which yielded an instant and immeasurable crop.

The ability to commune with nature while trudging through soil
and attending to the essentials of good farming meant everything to
him, so much that he harbored critical opinions of those who failed
to revere it. Such failure amounted to an attitude that working on a
farm translated only into a series of mundane and boring chores in
pursuit of a living for oneself or a mere grind in the struggle to provide for one's family, or—most horrid of all!—conducting a *business*
with only one goal in mind: the great god profit, an objective wholly
detrimental to nature's intended ways.

Men have become the tools of their tools, he insists in his journal. *But what is the use in trying to live simply, raising what you eat,*
making what you wear, building what you inhabit, burning what you
cut or dig, when those to whom you are allied insanely want and will
have a thousand other things which neither you nor they can raise
and nobody else, perchance, will pay for.

Expressing even more strongly his disdain for farmers who care
only about profit, he rails about their conducting *a war with the wil-*
derness [via] *breaking nature, taming the soil, feeding it on oats. The*
civilized man regards the pine tree as his enemy. He will fell it and
let in the light, grub it up and raise wheat or rye there. It is no better
than a fungus to him.

In his first book, *A Week on the Concord and Merrimack Rivers,*
he goes further, railing this time: *These modern ingenious sciences*
and arts do not affect me as those more venerable arts of hunting
and fishing, and even of husbandry in its primitive and simple form.
Ranting ever louder, he decries *avarice and selfishness, and a grov-*
eling habit, from which none of us is free, of regarding the soil as
property, or the means of acquiring property chiefly. The landscape is
deformed, husbandry is degraded with us, and the farmer leads the
meanest of lives. He knows nature . . . but as a robber.

HENRY FACTS

Given that Henry had such high regard for farmers, and was exceedingly adept at farming as well, why did he *not* go into farming as a profession? The answer seems to have come down to his greater calls to independence, curiosity, and adventure. Consider these passages from his journal:

> *The farmer has always come to the field after some material thing: that is not what a philosopher goes there for . . . Wealth will not buy a man a home in nature, [neither] house nor farm. The man of business does not by his business earn a residence in nature, but is denaturalized rather.*

At the same time, Henry greatly admired farmers who chose farming as a business for personal fulfillment versus only generating high profit margins. In that regard, he could emanate no greater praise than by comparing farming to the spiritual lives of American Indians, his mystical heroes. In his essay "Walking," he goes so far as to write: *I think that the farmer even displaces the Indian because [the farmer] redeems the meadow, and so makes himself stronger and in some respects more natural.*

From Henry, it don't come more laudatory than that!

FURTHER THOUGHTS
FROM HENRY ON FARMERS

When I witness the first plowing and planting, I acquire a long-lost confidence in the earth,—that it will nourish the seed that is committed to its bosom.

—Journal, 28 March 1857

How much Nature herself suffers from drought! It seems quite as much as she can do to produce these crops.

—Journal, 19 August 1851

I have faith that the man who redeemed some acres of land the past summer redeemed also some parts of his character.

—Journal, 1 March 1852

I sympathize with weeds perhaps more than with the crop they choke, they express so much vigor.

—Journal, 24 July 1852

I talked of buying Conantum once but for want of money we did not come to terms—but I have farmed it in my own fashion every year since.

—Journal, 31 August 1851

Write while the heat is in you. When the farmer burns a hole in his yoke, he carries the hot iron quickly from the fire to the wood, for every moment it is less effectual to penetrate it. It must be used instantly, or it is useless. The writer who postpones the recording of his thoughts uses an iron which has cooled to burn a hole with. He cannot inflame the minds of his audience.

—Journal, 10 February 1852

GAINING GROUND:
A PARTNERSHIP HENRY WOULD APPROVE

On the same acreage in Concord, Massachusetts, where Henry's birthplace house Thoreau Farm rests, a nonprofit farm, Gaining Ground, attends to a thirty-year mission to grow healthful food for individuals and families experiencing food insecurity via distribution to schools, food banks, free kitchens, and similar organizations in the surrounding areas. To fulfill this objective, Gaining Ground actively cultivates more than fifty organic vegetable and herb varieties in its fields, employing regenerative no-till farming practices with the aid of hundreds of student volunteers each year.

Given Henry's admiration of farming, especially a farm engaged in attempting novel and natural farming techniques that also integrate a social justice imperative, no organizational partnership that Henry could have devised himself could possibly be more suitable.

EXCERPT FROM HENRY'S "WILD APPLES"

In his essay on wild apples, Henry concludes with a lament: He fears they will ultimately disappear altogether, replaced by hemmed-in apple farms where fruit is available only at a price. No more climbing trees to pluck that gloriously tart prize once abundant here, there, and everywhere.

As one who grew up with my crab apple tree in a Massachusetts backyard only twelve miles (as the crow flies) from Henry's own yard, I concur with Henry's lament. Ours was one of the few such truly wild apple trees left in the area, just as Henry feared. Today none seem to be left at all, leaving u-pick-'em, then u-buy-'em private orchards as the only game left in northern New England. Thus Henry's initial line here is prophetic:

> The era of the Wild Apple will soon be past. It is a fruit which will probably become extinct in New England . . . I fear that he who walks over these fields a century hence will not know the pleasure of knocking off wild apples. Ah, poor man, there are many pleasures which he will not know.

Notwithstanding the prevalence of the Baldwin and the Porter, I doubt if so extensive orchards are set out to-day in my town as there were a century ago, when those vast straggling cider-orchards were planted, when men both ate and drank apples, when the pomace-heap was the only nursery, and trees cost nothing but the trouble of setting them out. Men could afford then to stick a tree by every wall-side and let it take its chance.

I see nobody planting trees to-day in such out-of-the-way places, along the lonely roads and lanes, and at the bottom of dells in the wood.

BUSINESS LESSON

I was not anchored to a house or farm, but could follow the bent of my genius every moment. Again Henry is emphasizing the high value of keeping things simple. Also, do not stray too far from nature or the farm or from birds, bees, forest critters, fish, plants—you name it! Preserve your freedom to "follow your bent," that is, best instincts and preferred choices toward how you spend your time. Life goes by quickly. Make the most of it *now*.

Grab your favorite #2 and pencil in your business lesson here:

_____

_____

_____

8

MASTER SURVEYOR

A day or two of surveying is equal to a journey.

For those somewhat or very familiar with Henry's professional life, his on-again, off-again occupation as a land surveyor has frequently been mentioned as the "only" way Henry ever really had found as a means of making some money. To an extent, this is exactly right, especially as Henry's preferred career as a poet, as well as his prose writing projects and speaking engagements tended to earn him only relatively meager financial rewards throughout his career. Had he been able to survive tuberculosis, which took him at the relatively young age of forty-five, he might've experienced *Walden*'s popularity growing by leaps and bounds.

In 1840, however, he began recalling some coursework on land surveying that he had taken back at Harvard and wondering if this might be a way to supplement his endeavors as a writer in general and a poet in particular. Though he was teaching at the Concord Academy at the time, presumably a stable revenue source, he may have doubted that teaching was "it" or possibly feared the school would close, as John had been increasingly ill that year. In any case, Henry seemed to sense more strongly than ever that surveying was something he should look at more closely.

But as a novice surveyor with no reputation, Henry faced the same challenge as anyone starting anew: proving himself. So instead of endlessly chasing every faint opportunity, he chose the performer's— creating his own "audition" through a bold, self-assigned challenge. He needed a major land surveying project, one impressive enough to showcase his skills.

But writing assignments—mostly from Waldo—occupied all his time for a few years. Potential projects, introductions, and false starts kept him distracted from his surveying "audition." Like so often in life, time slipped away, which prevented him from implementing this potentially great idea for far longer than he anticipated.

Then, finally, one cold winter's day in 1845, the backup returned, all bright and shiny and glistened up to go! Gazing out the window of his cabin toward Walden Pond one frigid morning, one can imagine the target of his pro bono audition becoming crystal clear: Where else? Walden Pond of course!

Stepping into his boots a few months later in winter 1846, then out into the frosty air, he likely set his sights on Walden's sixty-one acres of gleaming icy surface and legendary bottomless pit, certain that *this* location had been calling to him for a very long time. Henry had even remarked multiple times that some Concordians believed that Walden extended all the way down and through the center of the earth and then out the other side! Perhaps a chief goal of his audition might be to test that. Ridiculous or not, since no one else had ever measured from surface to bottom, why not he? *There's* a potential business project!

Though he couldn't know that it would be another three years until he obtained his first *paying* survey gig, he did feel in his bones that snowy day that one had to start somewhere. Now in the first January of his first year at Walden, the time had come, a lucky break bound solely by proximity. Henry put it succinctly in *Walden*: *I was desirous to recover the long lost bottom of Walden Pond,* [so] *I surveyed it carefully, before the ice broke up.*

Labor in the Open Air

Surveying Walden Pond was a challenge not for the faint of heart given its status as a so-called kettle pond, which many folks, irrationally, thought had no bottom. Kettle ponds form when a block of stagnant ice detaches from a glacier that slowly melts, leaving behind a pit. Water then begins filling the depression and forming a pond or lake, taking the shape of a kettle. As Patrick Chura, professor of English at the University of Akron, wrote in his book *Thoreau the Land Surveyor*, Henry had to therefore prove himself in several demanding ways: "Surveying Walden presented several significant technical challenges [and] it was also a physically arduous process requiring days and weeks of toil, some of it quite exhausting." He drilled more than one hundred "sounding holes" in ice sixteen inches thick, a feat that each time required "considerable cardiovascular stamina and physical power." This Harvard College grad and writer-woodsman needed to perform like an athlete especially as his methods of environmental inquiry, Chura notes, were "appropriately physical."

Amazingly, due to Henry's passion for this project, such hard work "did not blunt Henry's perceptions but [instead] stimulated his speculative and interpretive faculties, grounding an epistemology that was as much corporeal as cerebral. At Walden and after, labor in the open air was a source and basis of Thoreau's acute phenomenological discernment."

When all was said and done and his measurements of Walden Pond had been finally determined, Walden would prove to be the deepest "lake" in Massachusetts. Among other finds, this alone confirmed Henry's surveying expertise and reputation. The audition, in other words, was a success!

In 1849, when Concord commissioned Henry to survey Bedford Street for Waldo's proposed Sleepy Hollow Cemetery, he had firmly established himself as the town's go-to surveyor. This project launched his surveying practice, leading to a cascade of new commissions across neighboring towns—Lincoln, Bedford, Carlisle, and Acton—as well as diverse assignments:

- New streets near Concord's train depot
- Local farms and woodlots
- Area ponds and waterways
- Nathaniel Hawthorne's estate
- A cow barn
- A plan belonging to the Mill Dam Company
- Projects extending to Nantucket and Perth Amboy, New Jersey
- *All* bridges spanning the Concord River

The Concord Free Library's special collections documents his remarkable career with 165 surveyed properties, culminating in his ambitious "A Plan of the Public Lands in the State of Maine . . ." The sheer volume and variety of his work remains astonishing.

Thus the years stretching from his Walden audition through all the many subsequent projects skipped along, Henry appreciating more and more his ever-growing surveyor skills and viewing them less and less as a necessary income-generating evil. Surveying, it seemed, could be employed in a supportive role to his more passionate business aims, writing books, essays, and poems.

This represented a fresh perspective especially given his declaration in *Walden* that the mass of men had it backward:

Most men spend six days on a job for reasons of money only, and then rest on a seventh day, Sunday. Instead, that seventh day should be the one day in the week of a person's toil.

But despite his lessened hold on this sentiment, it remained true that his commitment to surveying, for much of his life, would never become quite like *that*, but remain instead a means to not only writing but also allowing him to make time for other avenues of expression, such as speaking presentations, nature walks, and simple saunters wherever he wished to roam. In fact, surveying provided him a means to double up on exploring, observing, recording, and analyzing whatever he might stumble upon, even if encountered while surveying a farmland or woodlot.

One such free moment brought him up close to a small, curious tiny mound of dirt in the middle of the path as he ambled along a forest trail. Bending down to look closer, his eyes fell upon tiny quick movements as if the ground itself was shifting this way and that. Bending closer, he realized he was on the edge of a "battleground" where hundreds of ants, split into red versus black "armies," engaged in fierce warfare with one another, combat not at all different from human soldiers intent on seizing—or defending—a strategic hilltop.

Marveling at this frenzied combat, he later described the raging enemy battalions this way:

I was witness to events of a less peaceful nature. One day when I went out to my woodpile, or rather my pile of stumps, I observed two large ants, the one red, the other much larger, nearly half an inch long and black, fiercely contending with one another. Having once got hold, they never let go, but struggled and wrestled and rolled on the "chips" on the ground incessantly.

Looking farther, I was surprised to find that the chips were covered with such combatants, that it was not a duellum, but a bellum, a war between two races of ants, the red always pitted against the black, and frequently two red ones to one black. The legions of these Myrmidons covered all the hills and vales in my woodyard, and the ground was already strewn with the dead and dying, both red and black.

It was the only battle which I have ever witnessed, and the only battlefield I ever trod upon while the battle was raging, internecine war; the red republicans on the one hand, and the black imperialists on the other.

By the time it was over and a victor had become clear, one can imagine Henry lifting himself up and brushing the dirt flakes off his pants, then moving along to his woodpile. Gazing up at the position of the sun, he realized how he'd been lying on the ground close to the action for a long time . . . in fact, for a *very* long time—four hours!

With the sun heading toward the evening sky, it would soon be dinnertime. Had he been taking a stroll during his lunch hour from Damon Mill, he would by now be three hours late for his afternoon shift. As an independent land surveyor, however, he could choose to grant himself this sort of freedom, an allowance that factory workers or millers or railroad conductors or storekeepers might view as frivolous in light of their workload . . . and quite possibly penalized by a dock in his pay or even by being fired by a supervisor.

Hanging Out His Shingle

Obviously the decision to go deeper into land surveying needed to mesh with Henry's absolute need to spend time in his life in whatever way he chose. It meant the difference for him between just getting by in life versus living a life that was *worth* living. Henry thus had apparently been drawn to surveying in part if not in whole because of two undeniable personal factors:

- **First, the most powerful draw for Henry was his love of nature**, along with his love of wandering, or "sauntering," through woodlands and high brush, up and down hilltops, and across rivers and streams, in support of his love of observing and analyzing nature and immersing himself in nature's *wonder*.

    Comparing one plant species to another, measuring bodies of water and topography, traversing inclines and ravines, all these enhanced the *scientific* side of his brain, enabling him to learn something new. Surveying enabled him to continue this while also earning him some money.

- **The second factor was his deeply ingrained independent streak.** Due to this propensity, Henry likely never even entertained the notion of applying for a *job* with a surveying company, preferring instead to acquire surveying knowledge on his own, applying his surveying "artistry" at his own pace to this totally new occupation. He would have known from deep down in his soul that he must go bravely into this unfamiliar endeavor alone.

So the entrepreneurial model was the only option for him. He had gotten his first taste of it when he opened their Concord Academy with his brother John and from then on felt it growing stronger and deeper within him, insisting that he recognize there was no other way. As an entrepreneur, he could choose which days to work, how many weeks to work, and how many days to work, what *times* of day to work, and even who his clients would be. No employee gets away with all that!

As well, to work as an employee would also mean temptation to betray his conscience. After a few years of land surveying, he had learned this was inevitable. He now knew that *most landowners want to cut corners so as to identify boundary lines that result in more land for him and thus more profit as opposed to doing the right thing.*

The thought of adhering to such a client/employer dynamic wherein one's boss could insist or *demand* that he conduct himself in a corrupt manner struck him as abominable. Particularly as the only probable reason for doing so might be to earn what would rightly be termed filthy lucre. The very thought of it always wrenched him back to that horrific episode when he'd been ordered by the Concord school administrator to keep his children attentive and well-behaved via the application of the lash and harsh invectives.

That day, surrendering his principles and carrying out such shameful actions had left him shattered. When he quit, he had vowed, "Never again." That moment may have planted the seed for his future entrepreneurial path—a firm resolve to never again endure such moral compromises in the workplace.

Thus hanging out his "shingle," as it were, set him not only on a track to self-apprenticeship and bit by bit to full-fledged self-employment but also toward a model of surveying conscientiousness unheard of in his own day and, to a great extent, our own. The key for Henry was to do surveying "right" versus merely pleasing his customer and collecting a fee. Right equaled morality *plus* compensation with both sides of this equation present in every situation.

But what else did "right" mean? To Henry it meant proceeding carefully, meticulously, and, often, slowly. It meant working above and beyond all expectations too as he measured "excessively"—Waldo's word—not only such projects as Walden Pond and the Concord River but whatever number of farmlands he agreed to survey as well.

So his objective would always be to determine the proper outcome for the land itself rather than a landowner client's hope for a tidy selling price and profit. His survey of Walden Pond affords one such example of how this sometimes played out as he plumbed the bottom of Walden several times at multiple points in both day and night. His continual measurement of the Concord River for a project commissioned by the town mildly annoyed Waldo as extravagant and unnecessary, at one point writing a friend that Henry "occupies himself with the history of the river [as he] measures it, weighs it & strains it through a colander to all eternity."

This thorough approach and high ethical standard, however, carried him through many years of successful projects to a high point where he became known not just for doing "good work" or "great work" but the "very best" work as compared to all his fellow surveyors hither or yon. This lifted him above his competition beyond Concord, steering him to a point where people could often think of no one else for certain projects except their local go-to. We *have* to get Henry for this one, why go with anyone else?

It was what I used to subscribe to before the arrival of the internet: "Get them to call you." I now articulate it slightly differently, i.e., "Get them to c*ontact* you" since almost nobody contacts us initially by phone anymore nor answers their own phone without first checking caller ID. Instead emails and texts and LinkedIn messages, to cite just a few, seem to be first steps for 99% of us. But the idea itself still rings true: Establish your value and spread the word in such a way that your prospective customers hear it and comprehend it, then seek *you* out rather than the other way around. Once you get prospects to contact you, they'll already be 50% or so in your corner, i.e., sold. Now you only have to drive them through the remaining 50% by persuading them you can indeed do what you have publicly claimed . . . and seal the deal!

The result was his hometown officially bestowing on Henry the title "Chief Surveyor of Concord." This honor put a cap on Henry's status as a pinnacle of business success!

Henry Surveys the Concord River

Attaining such a lofty go-to status, however, ultimately came about, once and for all, because of a particularly desperate need on the part of many Concord farmers whose farms were situated along the banks of the Concord River. A calamity had been growing for decades among these farms in an area then called the Concord Valley. The crisis had developed due to an ongoing industrialization of the river that in turn caused a swelling environmental adverse impact endangering these farmers' dependency on the river's natural flow.

Patrick Chura in his book *Thoreau the Land Surveyor* explains it this way: "What became known as the Concord River flowage controversy began in the late eighteenth century with the construction of the Middlesex Canal Dam in nearby Billerica, Massachusetts. In a series of lawsuits against the dam owners that began in 1811, the farmers owning meadows along the Concord River claimed repeatedly that because the dam slowed drainage, the river flooded more frequently and retained moisture longer following summer rains." The farmers thus argued as the crisis developed that their fields and meadows had grown "softer and wetter," repeatedly spoiling their "valuable crops of meadow hay," which the farmers counted on for livestock "winter fodder."

To make matters worse, Chura writes, when the river level fell and the meadow hay began to dry out in the summer months, the mill owners "opened their supply reservoir, flooding the meadows and spoiling the farmers' hay before it could be harvested." Flash-forward to Thoreau's injection into the standoff approximately fifty years later (yes, it had been going on that long!) where Henry encountered a riverscape that now included "dozens of textile and powder mills" all up and down the Concord River basin. The result of this was a flow rate under the control of the relatively new industrial interests "much to the detriment of farmers who had worked the area for generations."

So in 1859 the River Meadow Association (RMA) hired Henry to survey the river as the RMA looked toward its next legal case. In many respects this was a dream project for Henry not only because he might be able to settle this long-standing frustration for Concord's farmers but also because he had been wishing to undertake a survey of the Concord River for some time now, as a kind of nature study, even if he had to undertake it voluntarily as he had done at Walden Pond years before. Henry's goal was driven by his hope that such a survey might reveal, in his words, *that uncharted, unexplored part of the earth whose geography has never been mapped.*

So Henry dove in and did what he could, applying his thoroughness and 24/7 commitment to measuring and testing and sighting in a manner that only the best surveyors know how to do. And though I would love to write here that Henry saved the day, the actual answer is "not quite."

Ultimately the court, instead of siding with farmers despite Henry's Herculean efforts, ruled in favor of the industrial forces, citing a dubious standard that declared the farmers had "waited too long." This despite all the decades of litigation that had been going on. Though Massachusetts's legislature had at first sided with the farmers and ordered the dam removed and damages paid to the farmers, upon further investigation over the next two years, the same Massachusetts legislature reversed itself, decreeing that restoring the river and its banks would now require a massive reengineering project.

The hard reality of that meant, according to the legislature, that it was now just too late to carry out such an overwhelming, burdensome, and expensive commitment. One farmer, exasperated, testified at the trial that their precious river was now "dammed at both ends and cursed in the middle."

Even so, Henry's efforts had been hugely helpful to get the farmers to at least their initial victory, that earlier ruling in their favor by the legislature, an achievement due not only to his carefully measuring of the river day and night but also time spent sitting at home at his little desk with all his measurements and staring at them, thinking everything through, and appraising the enormous environmental havoc that had been growing bolder all these years.

So the town of Concord, understanding these circumstances, soon hired Henry again, this time to resume surveying the river all the way up and down, including charting it and measuring its bridges, the dream job he'd wished to initiate for many years.

Laura Dassow Walls characterizes how this played out this way: Henry paddled "every inch of [the river's] twenty-two miles, measuring depths and breadths, noting sandbars and shallows and potential obstructions." Walls added that "the more Thoreau worked, the more the data spoke to him of the river as a grand human-natural system."

Going above and beyond, with passionate extra care, as always, Henry elevated the stature of his surveying practice even more, ultimately racking up, at the end of his surveying career, sixty thousand acres of surveyed land and water. In terms of a scorecard, veteran surveyors have now confidently certified Henry an unbridled surveying success. Henry later in his life agreed, once proclaiming simply: *"I am a surveyor."*

GREAT MEADOWS
NATIONAL WILDLIFE REFUGE

Many years after the struggles of the River Meadow Association farmers in the Concord Valley played themselves out, the area would be converted into a wildlife habitat called the Great Meadows National Wildlife Refuge. Replete with walking trails, landscapes au naturel, duck ponds, and a wildlife observation tower, visitors can now enjoy nature in the same way Henry had at Walden Woods and Walden Pond, hiking, snowshoeing, bird-watching, cross-country skiing, canoeing, and of course, sauntering.

HENRY'S SURVEYING SKILLS:
SUCCESS TRAP OR LUCKY BREAK?

In 1851, Henry became Concord's chief surveyor, leading to his playing an essential role as an adjudicator in public and private controversies related to land ownership. In some ways, this might have felt to Henry like a yoke around his neck, an image that would have made sense to him and to everyone else involved in farming. Plowing a field, after all, had typically been accomplished with the strong, steady plodding of the day's current technology: a yoked oxen or two!

However, in a review in *The American Surveyor* magazine of Patrick Chura's book, Patrick C. Garner, a professional land surveyor for more than thirty-five years in Massachusetts, comments that Henry "was often subsumed by the beauty of the underlying geometry rather than the job itself," which likely saved him. For too many of us, moving up what is considered a ladder of success sometimes turns into something very different: a success trap!

This is typically due to what is called the Peter Principle, an impenetrable ceiling that keeps one in the same place, despite attaining the top rung of the success ladder. The idea is you can now go no higher! This means one may as well be facing a wide, high sign blocking your way and commanding: GO NO FARTHER! YOU HAVE REACHED THE LIMIT OF YOUR ADMIRABLE SKILLS! HERE YOU WILL STAY FOR THE REST OF YOUR CAREER. Alas . . . the success trap! You have done so well that you no longer have any new rungs to grab. You have succeeded so well that you now have nowhere else you can go.

Henry, however, seemed to have escaped this fate. Garner explains in his review of Patrick Chura's book how several authors and scholars in the past "have opined that Thoreau was in fact one of the premier surveyors of that period. But Chura convincingly makes the case that Henry achieved that rarified level because of his passion, honesty and his simple lifelong love of measuring."

In other words, "Thoreau the businessman excelled because he did not approach surveying as a business but as an art, learning the rudiments of surveying at Harvard and then teaching himself the advanced intricacies of the profession."

Garner then goes on to report that Chura attributes Thoreau's passion "to his love of orderliness and his natural attraction to the organization required of surveying. It was a necessary job as well since Thoreau too needed income—but it became a skill that reinforced his natural instinct to measure, observe and understand."

Garner wraps his review with this glowing verdict: "Chura's strength is in his emphasis on Thoreau's ethics. That high moral sensibility was characterized by Thoreau's neutrality, that is, he treated client and abutter equally, and by his obsession with accuracy regardless of his client's demands."

Q&A WITH PATRICK CHURA,
AUTHOR OF *THOREAU THE LAND SURVEYOR*

**Yours is a unique book on Henry David Thoreau in that it empha-
sizes his job life rather than the more usual spotlights of, for
example, environmentalism, civil disobedience, Walden Pond,
etc. You write in your preface that what initially inspired you to
tackle Thoreau in this particular way was a curiosity about how
Thoreau actually earned money.**

The mere thought of Thoreau earning money was already outside
the usual scope of most scholarly approaches. Yet it was a real factor
in the life of the "saint of the woods" as it is for nearly all of us. So
it was a legitimate question. And for Thoreau, who was as much a
natural scientist as a writer, it turned out to be important because
it combined his studies of the natural world with earning his living.

**Yet many people would see a contradiction in Henry the nature
lover and Henry the agent of property ownership, especially when
aimed at making a profit versus preserving the wild.**

Of course there's a downside to the process of lotting off wilderness
and abetting an ethos ownership and "property," clearly anathema
in some ways to Thoreau as proto-environmentalist thinker. But it's
clear that he did much to address this paradox, ultimately succeeding in "making meaning" of his work by repurposing it in productive and sometimes subversive ways. My book in fact has been given
credit by some as the impetus for what many have come to call a
"material turn" in Thoreau studies.

**What do you say to someone who asks what Henry did "for a liv-
ing," that is, do you respond simply "surveyor" or do you characterize his overall work life as more complex than that?**

I wouldn't say he was "a surveyor solely," of course, but in his later
years he sometimes said this himself, like when he was thinking of
earning his bread. Over time, I think he became comfortable with
it, saw its value—I liked that quote from him about "a day or two of

surveying is equal to a journey." It got him away from things so he could return to, for example, a book manuscript with fresh eyes. It was a way of "seeing" that he had honed through his practice and it was, I believe, an important tool that added value and insight to his writing.

Did anything surprise you from your research about Henry's work/ career/business practices that's not in the popular image of his life and persona?
Not really, because I knew a thing or two about surveying, but I do recall that when I submitted an initial article about the topic describing Thoreau sharpening wooden stakes and pounding them into the ground at Walden Woods, some scholars were shocked. "Are you *sure* he did this?" one asked me.

Well, of course he did this! The reason his survey notes say "stake and stones" at the lot corners is because he, as surveyor, pounded in a stake and arranged some field stones to mark the corner.

I will admit that I did not fully realize how *difficult* it was in Thoreau's day to get accurate numbers such as compass bearings, leveling operations, other measurements, especially using the crude equipment of the day to survey something as large as Walden Pond. I was also pretty amazed at how hard Thoreau worked for accuracy. He didn't always need to, but he did because, after all, he had very high standards!

How would you summarize Henry's attitude toward "work" in general?
He seemed to believe that if work was worth doing, it was always worth doing right. He seemed to recognize that this was how surveying became science, so why do it sloppily? Use it to at least *attempt* to penetrate nature's secrets or see something new. And he did see new things while surveying!

What lessons can business leaders glean from Henry's work practices?
He acquired trust and respect from clients because he saw his business task as full of dignity when done right. Measure the right way, even if the client would rather you fudge the numbers to give him more land and profit. Don't cut corners, not even to make the client happy.

> **BUSINESS LESSON**
>
> *What lies behind us and what lies ahead of us are tiny matters compared to what lives within us.* Henry's choice to find a way to serve his surveying customers in a manner that was win-win for everyone allowed him to sleep at night. Help your customers understand that you are sometimes doing the right thing even when it feels to them you should be doing more for them than a situation warrants. If you stand up for your principles in these moments, you will, like Henry, earn their trust even if met with temporary grumbling. Down deep, they will recognize you are doing the right thing and come back to you rather than replace you with your less-honest competition.

Grab your favorite #2 and pencil in your business lesson here:

_____

_____

_____

9

HENRY'S MARKETING PROWESS

*Only he is successful in his business who makes that pursuit
which affords him the highest pleasure sustaining him.*

In *Faith in a Seed,* one of his later writings, published posthumously, Henry wrote:

> *Though I do not believe that a plant will spring up where no
> seed has been, I have great faith in a seed . . . Convince me that
> you have a seed there, and I am prepared to expect wonders.*

Obviously, this sentiment was intended toward his view of how nature operates from start to finish, that the beginnings of it all emanate from the often tiniest seedling and then the mechanics of it all takes things from there, sometimes, many years later, generating a magnificent giant oak or sequoia tree.

But we might also view this remark as his view of a successful business's trajectory. You begin with an idea, a dream, a Big, Hairy, Audacious Goal—or BHAG as bestselling author Jim Collins labeled it in his mega-popular classic *Built to Last: Successful Habits of Visionary Companies.*

Henry articulated his thinking along these lines in this famous quotation: *If you have built castles in the air, your work need not be lost; that is where they should be. Now put the foundations under them.*

A telling tale in *Walden* about a local Indian in Concord attempting to sell homemade baskets expands on this, a development outlined in the following post "Thoreau's Definition of Marketing" by digital marketing expert Mark Whittaker who writes on his website www.markwhittaker.com:

It surprised me to find marketing advice while reading Henry David Thoreau's *Walden*. Although I know a little about Thoreau, an early nineteenth-century essayist, poet, and philosopher, I've never read *Walden*. The book is his most prominent work, which describes his life in a small, self-built cabin on Walden Pond in Concord, Massachusetts.

Early in the book, he tells a story about a local Native American who unsuccessfully tried to sell woven baskets to his wealthy, white neighbors. The man was upset and exclaimed: "What! Do you mean to starve us?"

It turns out, according to Thoreau, that the man had decided to make baskets because it was something he was able to do. *"Thinking that when he had made the baskets he would have done his part, and then it would be the white man's to buy them,"* Thoreau writes.

The man's logic was similar to that of modern entrepreneurs who often create products because they can, without considering whether anyone will buy them.

[But] Thoreau quickly gets to the root of the problem. The basket-maker, he writes, *"had not discovered that it was necessary for him to make it worth the other's while to buy them, or at least make him think that it was so, or to make something else which it would be worth his while to buy."*

Can you think of a better definition of business marketing?

"Build It and They Will Come?"

The moral of this story, of course, in Henry's view, would be that the process of creating and founding a successful business needs to encompass more than mere planning to offer the marketplace a product or service. Because instead the next step should involve conducting what we now refer to as "market research" to identify your ideal customer as well as determine what would constitute your prospective client's ideal *value* to convince them to fork over the price you are asking.

"Convince me!" Henry wrote, flinging those words at the Indian basket-seller Joe. "Convince me" that you have a seed there worth my while, then "convince me" to come your way toward a mutually satisfying transaction. Such a product pipeline begins with an appealing "idea," which graduates to "development" of your product idea, then on to "marketing research" to refine the ideal target market, then to marketing itself (i.e., getting the word out). Following this comes your sales pitch, then, ultimately and hopefully, finishing up with an actual sale. Simple enough action plan, right?

Well, yes and no. A well-worn quote from Henry is this one: *Our life is frittered away by detail. Simplicity, simplicity, simplicity!,* to which Waldo is rumored to have bemusedly remarked, "You know, Henry, *one* 'simplify' would've been enough!"

But this suggests business folk must beware of getting bogged down in detail as well as take care to keep each step along the road to success as simple as possible. Was it enough, for example, for basket-weaver Joe to *simply* stand on a Concord street corner and wave his pretty baskets for all to see, then expect customers to eagerly step right up and pull out their billfolds? Was that alone all that was needed to crank up the pipeline "buying engine" and ensure all of Joe's baskets got sold? Nope, never (or at least rarely) happens!

Then what else might have helped Joe make some sales? Would it have been better, for example, if Joe had designed some clever signage? Maybe a lively, colorful display of baskets on the street corner? Or another marketing ploy to "prime" his potential customers as they walked his way? Henry would likely have agreed that, yes, a marketing gambit or two might have helped.

In one of my previous business books, *The Expert's Edge: Become the Go-To Authority People Turn to Every Time*, I outlined what I call the "5 pillars of thoughtleading." In recognizing that Henry lived these pillars to the fullest, my verdict on Henry as a "certified" thoughtleader is clear because, truth be told, Henry seemingly well understood how much of his business success would depend on more than just knocking out a product or service idea; marketing and selling components were essential as well. Observe below my five pillars of thoughtleading and how they align perfectly with Henry's marketing sense.

Pillar #1: Publish Your Ideas

Henry's dream career, as we discussed in earlier chapters, was to make his living as a poet and/or writer. Though relatively little income ever came his way from either of these career goals during his lifetime, he nevertheless managed to publish approximately two hundred poems in a wide range of journals in addition to two books and multiple essays, some of them ultimately published in book format after his death.

The purpose of this pillar, publishing your ideas, is twofold: Get your ideas out into the marketplace so they can be examined by your buying public and by third-party reviewers and endorsers. This sets the stage for the pillar's second purpose (i.e., for potential buyers to come *seeking* your product or service rather than you searching for new customers like a needle in the haystack).

Pillar #2: Speak to Groups

Although not a sought-after public speaker the likes of Waldo, who typically spent four to six months a year traveling to speaking gigs in other US towns and states, as well as across Europe, Henry none-theless spoke many times in towns around Concord like Boston, Worcester, Nantucket, New Bedford, and Lowell, as well as in Rhode Island, New Hampshire, Connecticut, Pennsylvania, and New Jersey.

In doing so, he expanded his contacts while sharing his ideas. Subsequently, attendees could then go out and spread the word about his books, essays, and poems, presumably resulting in book sales and even land surveying assignments and/or sales of Thoreau pencils.

Pillar #3: Fresh Thinking

If Henry was good at anything, it was fresh thinking! No one could hold a candle to his observations, analyses, and conclusions, whether they ended up in his published works or in his many daily journals (think *blog* here!) that ultimately amounted to a life total of two million words. Fresh thinking like this would end up integrated into his land survey projects and his reinvention of the pencil, just two of the many astonishing business advances Henry orchestrated. Fresh thinking or counterintuitive ideation knows few bounds when called upon to adapt to life challenges, dilemmas, and crises. Henry was a master at it.

Pillar #4: Creatively Leverage the Internet

Now, okay, okay, I get it . . . no internet existed in Henry's day, right? Of course not, so mea culpa, mea culpa.

But what about the "internet" of Henry's time? Yes, I'm talking means and methods for circulating ideas virally, such as newspapers, books, journals, advertisements, broadsides. And of course, all those letters people used to write to each other, the staff of life that histori-ans feed on today!

If email marketing still leads the pack in our crazy epoch of X, Bluesky, Zoom, Truth Social, Instagram, Facebook, YouTube, Tik Tok, etc.—and, according to most research, it *does*!—wouldn't letters suffice as a means for Henry to "creatively leverage technology" in the mid-1800s and spread the good news of his expertise far and wide?

Certainly Henry secured numerous speaking engagements as well as writing assignments for publications and book reviews (due to books sent directly by Henry) with help from the good ole US mail.

Pillar #5: Vigorous Use of the Media

Similar to Pillar #4, our media today puts the mass media in Henry's day to shame. Except for the recently invented telegraph, there was no "online" nor much media technology back then to speak of. So what "vigorous" use of media was possible?

Well, advertising did exist, both in the newspapers of the day and via wall posters and handbills. In his book, Patrick Chura conducts a brilliant analysis of a well-known Henry broadside, that is, a large advertisement typically pasted *broadly across the side* of a wall. Here's a summary of Chura's breakdown of that broadside with commentary from both Patrick and myself.

HENRY: **Land Surveying**
PATRICK: A surprisingly slick marketing message that announced his availability for surveying "of all kinds."
KEN: Big and bold and centered and an uppercase heading right there at the top blaring that, if excellence in land surveying was something you might be looking for by an expert who can handle all your surveying needs, you've come to the right place!

HENRY: **. . . Of all kinds, according to the best methods known:**
PATRICK: Here Henry boldly asserts that he is capable of delivering "all kinds" of "the best methods known." This advert spotlights

LAND
SURVEYING

Of all kinds, according to the best
methods known; the necessary data supplied, in order that the boundaries of
Farms may be accurately described in
Deeds; *Woods* lotted off distinctly and
according to a regular plan; *Roads* laid
out, &c., &c. **Distinct and accurate Plans
of Farms furnished,** with the buildings
thereon, of any size, and with a scale of feet
attached, to accompany the Farm Book, so
that the land may be laid out in a winter
evening.

Areas warranted accurate with almost
any degree of exactness, and the Variations
of the Compass, so that the lines can be run
again.   Apply to

HENRY D. THOREAU
near the depot
Concord Mass.

This broadside is a customized version updated for easy reading.

Henry's goal of differentiating himself from his competition via tech-
nologically advanced methods and precision.
KEN: The words in bold are Henry's bold, placed on their own lines
so as to catch the eye and keep the focus on the remaining words of
a sentence ("methods known"), thus not be missed.

HENRY: . . . the necessary data supplied, in order that the
boundaries of Farms may be accurately described in Deeds;
PATRICK: Here the ad defines the "market niche" that Henry seeks to
fill, which is a particular type of surveying required around Concord

known as "metes-and-bounds." An example is found in an 1851 survey Henry conducted where he describes a parcel as *beginning at the northeasterly corner in the middle of a ditch on the pond*. Such use of natural or even man-made objects in the course of a survey contrasts with the standard geometrical grid approach.

HENRY: . . . **Woods lotted off distinctly and according to a regular plan**
PATRICK: This marketing appeal appears to have been particularly well-timed and effective, accounting for a large number of jobs of this type over the course of his career.
KEN: Henry didn't want to throw away any projects better suited to the less-inventive methods, especially those given to neat and orderly subdivisions of woodlots, lest he leave too much money on the table. So, though many of these had as their ultimate outcome the cutting down of trees so that the farmer might make extra revenue by selling off timber, Henry the businessman was astute enough to recognize that this service too should be articulated.

HENRY: . . . **Roads laid out, etc., etc.**
PATRICK: The reference here to "Roads laid out, etc., etc." seems to be in a similar category as Woods above, referring as it does to Henry's role in building the Concord area's transportation infrastructure. Road surveying and civil engineering projects emanated more and more from what became his most lucrative client, the town of Concord, which rehired him frequently throughout the 1850s, ultimately appointing him the official town "Chief Surveyor."

HENRY: . . . **Distinct and accurate Plans of Farms furnished, with the buildings thereon, of any size, and with a scale of feet attached, to accompany the Farm Book.**
PATRICK: This reference to the "Farm Book" was significant in that this was a kind of journal kept by landowners that included financial data, records of crops and harvests and information about the physical property. In referencing the Farm Book, Henry was

communicating that such data would provide a permanent record that would safeguard one's holdings by forestalling boundary disputes and encroachments. Security in one's property thus represented "added value" from a survey by Henry Thoreau.

HENRY: . . . so that the land may be laid out in a winter evening.
PATRICK: Here the diction suddenly achieves a lyrical tinge, creating an appealing pastoral image that would not be out of place in the pages of *Walden*. By means of both practical and emotive appeal, offering security and the full realization of the American form of autonomous land ownership, the author of this broadside is selling nothing less than the American Dream.
KEN: There is something reflective and un-businesslike in this final statement, an extra-added benefit that ties together all the other wonderful reasons to hire Henry. Laid out in a "winter evening" . . . was that even a thing? Yet there it is in all its sublime, seasonal splendor. Go light up a fire in your hearth, light up your corn-cob pipe, boil up some hot chocolate. All is well both inside and outside on this snowy winter evening . . . Henry is handling it!

HENRY: . . . Areas warranted accurate within almost any degree of exactness,
PATRICK: Here Thoreau employs standard advertising hyperbole, reiterating his slogan-like opening "according to the best methods known."
KEN: Just to be sure, Henry adds an ironclad promise. What could be more business-y? Harkening back to the top, he assures all broadside readers of his commitment to surveying with excellence. Folks, I personally guarantee your satisfaction!

HENRY: . . . and the Variations of the Compass given, so that the lines can be run again.
PATRICK: Such information would have been more helpful to future repeat surveys of the land parcel rather than of immediate use to clients, yet again Henry suggests here that he can offer benefits not

available from his competition due to skills he has developed on his own that enable him to customize variations of his surveys.

HENRY: Apply to HENRY D. THOREAU
KEN: Note Henry's name entirely in upper case here! How can you miss it?

HENRY: . . . near the depot, Concord Mass
KEN: Short and sweet and homey. Just wander over to the railroad depot located conveniently near Henry's mom's boardinghouse where he lives with his family in a yellow house known all around Concord. You can't miss it!

Also, this looks like an afterthought given it's written in script. Probably added when Henry realized the broadside didn't offer any info about how to locate him! So of course . . . he fixed it!

FINAL NOTE FROM PATRICK: That Thoreau knew what his customers wanted and how to appeal to them is clear from this broadside. Viewing the surveyor of Walden Pond as an economic man is not only accurate, it increases his relevance to the present day. Overall, this advertising broadside is an uncharacteristic piece of Thoreau's writing, but it should not be ignored as a literary text. It reminds us of the author's technical abilities and shows how his writing skills could be, and were, tailored to business conditions in shrewd and effective ways.
FINAL NOTE FROM KEN: Ditto!
FINAL NOTE FROM HENRY: *I am a surveyor!*

BUSINESS LESSON

Goodness is the only investment that never fails. In promoting himself, Henry made it clear that he could do for them what most of his competitors could not. But no false claims here, no desperate gimmicks, no bait-and-switch. Lay out your expert and admirable qualities and customers will beat a path to your door. Then be sure to do what you have advertised. That's how to keep customers coming back again and again for the life of your business.

Grab your favorite #2 and pencil in your business lesson here:

_____

_____

_____

10

HENRY THE
SCIENTIST-NATURALIST

We can never have enough of nature.

E ven though the word *scientist* wasn't coined until 1834, Laura Dassow Walls, in *Material Faith: Thoreau on Science*, points out that Henry had long before then embarked on identifying himself, and behaving, as a *"true man of science."* He took issue, however, with the emerging scientific establishment's insistence on detached observation. His contemporaries feared that personal engagement might bias their assessments, potentially leading to inflated claims about new discoveries—whether plants, animals, or insects.

To Henry, however, this was unthinkable. To proceed under this assumption would tamp down one's instinctive "fresh thinking," diminishing one's capacity to appreciate how the wondrously diverse and mysterious world actually worked. For Henry, human interaction was not a barrier but crucial to understanding *anything* and *everything*!

The true man of science, he wrote in his journal, *must be brave and sympathetic rather than objective or impersonal. Only in this manner could a deeper and finer experience emerge, drawing upon "Indian wisdom."* Continuing in this vein, he added that *the sum of what the writer of whatever class has to report is simply some human experience, whether he be poet or philosopher or man of science. The man of most science is the man most alive, whose life is the greatest event.*

This was all fully in line with Henry's view that combining a poet's perspective with the tenets of science was the only acceptable means of producing genuine scientific value. No, it was not enough to stand back and just observe. It was instead essential to also peruse and muse and effuse and enthuse. How else could one learn the secrets of nature if not by carefully dismantling an abandoned bird's nest, or pulling off a branch from a tree to learn how things looked *inside* the branch, or monitoring such natural everyday occurrences as the meanderings of a garter snake, the rummaging of an eagle on high, the gyrations of a muskrat in thick brush below?

Henry's perspective called into question even the acceptability of long-held practices like taxidermy or picking a bouquet of flowers from a field so as to drop them inside a vase. Why shoot to kill a wise old owl or busy beaver or exquisite blue heron, then stuff them for display on a shelf rather than spending an afternoon following them around and recording their movements and habits? Wouldn't human observation of animal behavior yield more scientific knowledge than bringing a wondrous animal's life to a halt?

As for even the prettiest of flowers, as great as they are for brightening up one's home or workplace, what becomes of all these flowers' accompanying natural life that gets left behind? Think of all the grasses, shrubs, trees, swamplands, insects—you name it! How much more might the naturalist gain from attending to all these as well? Why are weeds, for example, automatically second-class citizens? Or worthy of only getting yanked from the ground, then discarded? Yes, Henry felt strongly that even paying attention to weeds could prove essential.

Then there's Henry's statements that placed poets on the same rung as the *philosopher or man of science*. Walls explains this by citing Henry's *positive ideal* of viewing a poet as one who could unite earth and sky, thus melding science and philosophy, and generalizing *their widest deductions to cross the chasm between knowledge and ignorance through one's own practical experience in the world. The poet would then turn science into con-science, [giving life to] a moral knowledge.*

Questions became Henry's core tools, lack of understanding a failure to take action. From this productive interplay of increased knowledge and challenges to ignorance, Walls summarizes that Henry "derived his oft-repeated advice to 'learn science and then forget it,' coupling ever-present hypothesis with science knowledge, in which every yea must reserve a nay for the morrow."

The First Professional Nature Writer

Beyond all this, or maybe because of it, Henry has been deemed one of the first, perhaps even the very first, professional nature writer. No less an authority in this area than the late sociobiologist E. O. Wilson gave him this label, inserting an extra laudatory adjective—*great*—in recognition of Henry's talent as both a science observer and a "lyrical expositor" whose knowledge of the living world, based on experience, was "refined and projected as poetry."

Wilson also stated that "nature writing, one of the major innovations of American literature, includes in its pantheon John Muir, Aldo Leopold, and Rachel Carson. Together such writers agree with Henry's insistence that humanity co-evolved with the rest of life on our little planet such that people are deluded when they believe we humans can exist—let alone flourish—apart from the rest of our vibrant living world." Certainly Henry's thoughts and writings almost two centuries earlier contributed to Wilson's thinking and likely that of those members of the science-naturalist pantheon he listed.

Ongoing Walden Pond Census

Time spent at Walden Pond plus time spent wandering around Concord or canoeing down the Concord River or sauntering through Walden Woods certainly afforded Henry ample attention to nature, large or small. This was not pure entertainment of course—no matter how entertaining it was to Henry—but more active journeys into intellectual fulfillment. When he began inputting the details of all that he observed in the natural world into his daily journal, he unknowingly set the stage for ongoing scientific exploration that would live on well past his years.

To this day, perhaps the most visible manifestation of this is the troop of Boston University students that trek to Walden Pond each spring on a field trip to record the arrival of specific plants and flowers, then compare what they've found to Henry's journal notes. This yearly assignment is conducted by BU professor Richard Primack, author of *Walden Warming: Climate Change Comes to Thoreau's Woods*, who writes in an essay published in *What Would Henry Do, Volume I:* "In the late 1850s, Henry David Thoreau observed the first flowers on Concord's wild blueberry shrubs in the middle of May. Now Concord residents see blueberry flowers in April, three to six weeks earlier than Thoreau." This shift, Primack explains, denotes "the decline and disappearance of well-known wildflowers in Concord," likely due to climate change. In a profound full-circle moment, these modern field trips continue the solitary observations Henry first began nearly 170 years ago.

"Roughly one-quarter of the plant species that Henry saw in his wanderings around Concord's woods and wetlands are no longer there," Primack writes. "The changes we see in the climate and environment of Concord are a local version of the changes happening worldwide."

Primack's students thus pay homage to Henry with this outdoor project by committing to continuing it ad infinitum. In the face of a likely impending environmental catastrophe, however, the current Walden Pond census seems to be warning us that, despite his best efforts, Henry could never have sensed where the project's results of nature would indicate we are heading.

Henry Versus Louis Agassiz

In addition to Henry's pioneering the earliest days of science-naturalism, today's professional scientist-naturalists also owe a debt to Henry for even bucking the so-called greatest minds of his time when called for. In one case, this occurred at the peak of one such greatest mind's popularity and credibility, specifically that era's world-renowned Swiss scientist Louis Agassiz. Recognized for his thousand-page published books and for lectures to hundreds of attendees in various cities and universities, Agassiz's expertise ran the gamut of animals to fish to birds to plants. He could explain how each species had developed, the makeup of their anatomies, each species' particular habits, food sources, life spans. Educated and uneducated alike were enthralled by his lectures.

In 1846, Agassiz was invited to teach at Harvard and Boston's Lowell Center, so for a time, Henry contacted him to offer whatever support he could to Agassiz's explorations and theories. In response, Agassiz wondered if Henry could supply him with live animal and plant species that Henry might track down at Walden Pond.

Excitedly agreeing to this, Henry would capture a requested species if he could, then ship it off to Agassiz, which delighted and sometimes astounded the famous scientist. The fact was that in many cases Agassiz had never actually seen a particular critter or plant up close and thus was amazed, and grateful, to receive such specimens from Henry. "Study nature, not books," Agassiz once said, words that often seemed to be his motto. Yet actually examining various natural "objects" up close frequently escaped him. Henry therefore filled a gap for him like no one else in Agassiz's world ever could.

For a long while, Henry performed this service for Agassiz from afar, not getting the chance to come into Boston and meet him in person. The day came however when Henry finally came face-to-face with Agassiz at an intimate dinner at none other than Waldo's house. Waldo, who seemed to know *everybody*, was an inveterate match-maker and felt certain these two "greatest minds" would hit it off.

Alas, it was not to be. Although Henry at first was very enthused to meet Agassiz, the dinner discussion turned sour as they debated how the world's inhabitants came to be what they were and how they got there. On the question of the origin of all the species, Henry and Agassiz took marked issue. Though the exact dialogue was never recorded, we can imagine it going this way:

"Trees and plants and animals and insects and birds and fish—all life really—had been created by God himself," Agassiz assured his dinner companions. "And God placed each where it might be found to reside."

This was in direct opposition to the fresh thinking of the latest greatest mind on the scene, the scientist-naturalist Charles Darwin, whom Henry greatly admired.

But Agassiz would not hear of Darwin's wild, impossible theory, continuing that "if a type of turtle is found on the top of, say, the Andes Mountains, while a different type of turtle is found on some flatlands, each could get to where they were found only one way: by the miraculous hand of God. There could be no other explanation."

But Henry ventured to disagree, citing Darwin's new theory of evolution, which made a lot of sense to him, insisting that was another explanation, and a good one.

Agassiz then likely countered with a mini-lecture on the differing "species" of mankind. "Caucasian humans, for example," he intoned. "Are we not a sort of 'cream of the crop'? We are more intelligent, resourceful, creative, moral, and sensitive than other hominins such as those from Africa with black skins." Such primitive humanoids, he went on, were vastly inferior to the white-skinned variety, making it perfectly acceptable to own them and use them as we wish as slaves and servants.

As comments of this sort burst forth, Henry and Agassiz came to full-out loggerheads over the issue. Obviously this God-ordained white men's dominance was for Henry a bridge too far. The air remained cold for the rest of the dinner.

In the end, holding his ground, Henry finally brought back a little light. Maintaining his own theory of his "faith in a seed," specifically that a seed needs to be present for a flower or tree to eventually grow at that spot, rather than the result of a "spontaneous" planting process directed by God, Agassiz, perhaps inexplicably, chose to see Henry's point. Though jousting a bit with Henry at first, Agassiz ultimately agreed that this made sense, elevating Henry in Agassiz's mind to a higher rung of scientific thinking ability than Agassiz had previously been willing to admit.

How does the old saying go? The greatest minds think alike?

BUSINESS LESSON

As it is important to consider nature from the point of view of science, it is equally important to forget all that men presume they know. Life is always throwing us curve balls as an invitation to learn new things. Keep from shackling yourself to long-standing ideas born yesterday and patterns of behavior you figured out years ago. Lifelong learning is a great thing! But hold back from skepticism until you've heard and, even better, tried something brand-new. You might be shocked when you see that it works!

Grab your favorite #2 and pencil in your business lesson here:

_____

_____

_____

11

PUBLIC SPEAKER AND EVENT ORGANIZER

Thaw with his gentle persuasion is more
powerful than Thor with his hammer.
The one melts the other but breaks in pieces.

It has always struck me as odd that Henry, unlike myself and other professional author/speakers I have known, in modern times, typically conducted his writing/speaking process in an opposite format than I have come to assume is the more natural approach. For Henry, speaking always came first, while the norm that everyone else I have ever encountered follows has been "write first, speak later."

The logic behind "write first, speak later" insists that quietly gathering one's thoughts by thinking and reflecting, then putting an order to them in the form of an essay, article, or book liberates our brains to then be better able to articulate them out loud. At that point, whether through a one-to-one dialogue or small group or large audience, there might be a give-and-take that enables the writer/speaker to refine thoughts previously arranged by writing them out, and perhaps then go back and tweak or edit portions of the written words, thus clarifying them further, not only for those readers or audience attendees but for the writer/speaker as well.

The beauty of this lies in the likelihood that an audience's reaction to your spoken communication will *not* dictate that 100% of the earlier written expression must be changed but rather only smallish chunks of it. The heavy lifting of thinking through how to write about it usually—though not always!—saves the day by communicating the majority of the argument clearly enough that most of a speaker's treatise will attain a certain level of clarity and thus make sense.

Henry referred to his reverse process as "winnowing." As he once wrote in his journal: *From all points of the compass from the earth beneath and the heavens above have come these inspirations and been entered duly in such order as they came in the Journal. Thereafter when the time arrived they were winnowed into lectures—and again in due time from Lectures into Essays.*

Henry's approach was thus to make a note in his journal about something worth exploring further, then begin that process by writing out a lecture to be followed by trying it out on an audience, not winging it really but testing it to see how it would fly. He would then take the experience of communicating and responding to feedback back to his writing desk to set it in a prose form meant to be *read* rather than spoken. His "speak first, write later" method let him hone ideas through performance before perfecting them on the page.

Thoreau scholar Walter Harding explained it this way: "Delivering [was] part and parcel of Henry's authorship, directing him to write with audiences and the sound of words in mind, and, upon presentation, allowing him to hear himself think out loud and observe others' reactions to what he had to say."

Fortunately, Harding added, "Those reactions—whether newspaper reports or comments in letters and diaries—both before and after the publication of *Walden*, indicate that Thoreau, more often than not, was well received by a significant portion of his audience and that many of his lectures drew enthusiastic responses from an apparent majority."

But despite such an enthusiastic "significant portion of his audience," Harding also admitted that this did not ensure that Henry did not "lack for critics and outright detractors." All too often at least a few in his audiences expressed difficulty with his platform style and speaking voice. It's easy to imagine, for example, Henry coming off too much like a country bumpkin of some kind, so in love was he with nature, hometown, simplicity, and sauntering.

In contrast, many attendees might find him too far afield in another way: esoteric and hard to understand. In other words, for many in his audiences, his delivery could easily have been read as uber-idealistic and irrelevant to most folks' day-to-day lives, even at times arrogant and elitist, especially when he grew impatient with an attendee's question or argumentativeness.

"In an age of platform eloquence, when most of the lecture engagements went to the most engaging lecturers," Harding tells us, "Thoreau may be said to have suffered from an occupational disability. While Henry did enjoy some productive years and seasons as a lecturer, he never became a popular platform figure."

This "age of platform eloquence" of course drew from the reality that our more entertainment-oriented culture today had not yet arrived anywhere in Henry's world nor would it for at least another seventy or eighty years. For sure, back then, attending a guest lecture, even for poorly educated farmers, sheepherders, and storekeepers, offered a refreshing night out, a break from back-breaking workdays, not to mention an opportunity for a different sort of entertainment. For that reason, the quality of a speaker's "platform eloquence" was the key factor in the speaker leaving the lecture hall with a heavy hatful of silver half-dimes, buffalo nickels, twenty-cent pieces, and the occasional greenback—and best of all, an invitation to return the next year to speak again!

Fact-Check on Henry's Speaking Business

Despite questions regarding Henry's level of platform eloquence, Henry was indeed a professional speaker, which is to say he was actually paid for many of his speaking engagements and reimbursed for his travel expenses as well. Though he would never be, in terms of demand or pay, Waldo's equal (or Fredrick Douglass's, Sojourner Truth's, or Mark Twain's), he did nonetheless plod along. The facts speak for themselves:

- Years as a professional speaker: 23
- Total number of speaking gigs: 75
- Average number of speaking gigs per year: 3
- Typical speaking fee: $10–$20
- Total earned from speaking: $850+ (over 23 years)
- Average speaking income per year: $37

These were decent numbers considering that many speakers received much less (or nothing at all) from their attempts to generate *any* kind of speaking success. But behind these numbers lie deeper insights into Henry's approach—and valuable business lessons for today. Consider:

1. Henry's speaking business also brought him, for a few years, a paying position with the Concord Lyceum, where he was hired to serve as a meeting planner. However, he didn't last that long at it, probably because sitting at a desk all day and writing letter after letter wasn't the best fit for him. He likely spent too many moments staring out the Lyceum's window, wishing he could trudge on out of there, saunter over to Walden Woods, and just disappear!

But his association with Lyceum members and his fresh thinking may have been what led to the offer for the position. Lyceum management may have felt that he would be the best person to bring great speakers into Concord each year to fill up its programming.

2. He probably stayed away from asking for advice even from Waldo, despite Waldo's status as a renowned speaker both in the United States and Europe. Although Waldo, Horace Greeley, Bronson Alcott, and others continually recommended him for speaking gigs,

Henry's instinct may have been fending off mostly negative feedback rather than seeking out constructive criticism from allies, due to his solitary nature.

The following journal entries may help illuminate this, as they tell the tale of his not-so-diplomatic reactions to unsolicited criticism:

> *Generally, if I can only get the ears of an audience, I do not care whether they say they like my lecture or not . . . The stupidity of most of these country towns, not to include the cities, is in its innocence infantile.*
>
> *I am disappointed to find that most that I am and value myself for is lost, or worse than lost, on my audience. I fail to get even the attention of the mass. I should suit them better if I suited myself less . . .*
>
> *Many will complain of my lectures that they are transcendental. "Can't understand them." . . . But the fact is, the earnest lecturer can speak only to his like.*
>
> *Talk about reading!—a good reader! It depends on how he is heard. There may be elocution and pronunciation (recitation, say) to satiety, but there can be no good reading unless there is good hearing also. It takes two at least for this game.*
>
> *Always you have to contend with the stupidity of men. It is like a stiff soil . . . The stupid you have always with you . . . Read to them a lecture on "Education," . . . and they will think that they have heard something important, but call it "Transcendentalism," and they will think it moonshine.*

So though we all may have similar reactions when dealing with difficult individuals and even what seems like an entire audience—what Rodney Dangerfield used to label, on the old Johnny Carson *Tonight Show*, "tough crowd, Johnny, tough crowd"—Henry was obviously not given to summoning up much patience with any such conflicts. This alone may have hampered the development of his "platform eloquence"!

3. Finally, when all was said and done, Henry missed his days of four-hour walks around Concord and over to Walden Pond, Sandy Pond, White Pond, and the like, even in winter, and maybe especially in winter. Time spent building a lecture, then preparing and rehearsing it, then traveling to a speaking venue, then delivering the lecture, then roiling from the burn of unsolicited feedback or their ennui, while seated and exhausted on a train back to Concord—all of it, to Henry, was time driven out of a life that he always so loved and might never get back.

Walter Harding summed up this issue by quoting a journal entry of Henry's that exhibited his rueful lament: "The issue of winters lost to lecturing is recurrent, especially during the first lecturing season after *Walden*. Of his 6 December 1854 train ride to Providence, where he would lecture that evening, he remarked, *I see thick ice and boys skating all the way to Providence, but know not when it froze. I have been so busy writing my lecture.*"

Two days later, Harding informs us, Henry would complain again, writing forlornly:

Winter has come unnoticed by me, I have been so busy writing. This is the life most lead in respect to Nature. How different from my habitual one! It is hasty, coarse, and trivial, as if you were a spindle in a factory. The other is leisurely, fine, and glorious, like a flower. In the first case you are merely getting your living; in the second you live as you go along.

Henry's STL and TAL

In one of my previous books, *The Speaker's Edge: The Ultimate Go-To Guide for Locating and Landing Lots of Speaking Gigs,* originally published by Maven House Press, I laid out two basic tools all speakers must carry forward to a successful ongoing speaker business. These two essential tools are a Speaker Topics List (STL) and a Target Audience List (TAL). Henry took care to develop both. His STL looked like this:

- Slavery in Massachusetts
- Wild apples
- Moonlight
- Moose hunting
- A plea for Captain John Brown
- The last days of John Brown
- Martyrdom of John Brown
- The Maine woods
- The succession of forest trees
- Huckleberries
- A history of myself

And his TAL looked like this:

- Eager learners
- Readers
- Educators
- Farmers
- Storekeepers
- Students
- Professionals (doctors, attorneys, finance managers)
- Philosophers and deep thinkers
- Teachers
- Politicians
- Citizen activists

This list may seem vague and generalized as if to say that, well, his TAL consisted of everybody and anybody. Which in some ways is true, especially because what was likely on Henry's mind was that he welcomed anyone who wanted to learn and grow, especially those who showed up with an open mind. Thus his entire list might be boiled down to the first category, "eager learners."

Today, business-oriented speakers are more particular, focusing on audiences that would be best able to remunerate them for their appearances in the form of speaker fees, travel reimbursement, and additional revenue from consulting and/or training projects following a presentation. Thus a modern-day TAL might instead consist of one or more groupings like these: CEOs, COOs, CPAs, CFOs, HR managers, IP attorneys, sales managers, business developers and Thoreauvians (hah!), and so forth.

But for Henry, in a world where a speaker coming to town meant an excuse for locals of all stripes to come out and "see what this fella has to say," speakers focusing on virtually any topic had to take their chances that a substantial number of those local folks who came through the door would quietly sit, listen, and ask questions earnestly, then go home to ponder what this fine fellow (or "little lady") had to say.

As we have seen, for Henry things didn't always work out that way, but on the other hand, as Walter Harding has told us: "The [overall] reactions—whether newspaper reports or comments in letters and diaries—both before and after the publication of *Walden*, indicate that Thoreau, more often than not, was well received and that many of his lectures drew enthusiastic responses from an apparent majority."

Thus a large enough swath of Henry's audiences seemed to absorb his unique ideas, gushed over his observations, opinions, and stories, chuckled at his occasional quips and "foolishness," and all in all left the Lyceum or meeting hall appreciative and expressing good wishes that they would see him again in next year's lecture series.

Transcendentalism's Truest Advocate?

The bare facts of Henry's *positive* speaking engagements may have actually pointed to an even larger "win" for Henry whenever he connected with an audience, perhaps even outdistancing Waldo's moments of connection. Another way to say this is that Henry in some ways may have been transcendentalism's truest and most effective advocate when all the cards were counted. Lawrence Buell, author of numerous books on transcendentalism and American studies, and the Powell M. Cabot Professor of American Literature Emeritus at Harvard, writes about this in his latest book, *Henry David Thoreau: Thinking Disobediently*, published by Oxford University Press:

> To understand how Transcendentalism served as a launching pad that enabled Thoreau's reach to surpass Emerson's, consider Thoreau's engagements with two preeminent idols of the Transcendentalist tribe: reverence for nature and for unlimited human potential. In each case, Thoreau gave lasting embodiment to a sketchy model and recast it so distinctively that his versions became the seminal exempla.

Transcendentalist assertions of human divinity, Buell explains, were "long on dream but short on implementation." He quotes none other than Bronson Alcott, Lousia May's dad, and a prime voice in those heady days of hope for utopian dreams, as maintaining that "the mission of this Age, [was] to 'reproduce Perfect Men.'" But *his* exempla were confined to anecdotes of schoolchildren coaxed to express their higher promptings.

Waldo too offered "general recipes for self-transformation via contemplation of nature and resistance of conventional expectation." Other transcendentalist leaders, Buell explained, such as Theodore Parker, spoke of accessing the "great truth" of morality and religion "intuitively and by instinct" rather than via theology. Orestes Brownson, Henry's mentor back in Canton, Massachusetts, urged grand schemes for uplifting humanity by demolition and reconstruction of the whole socioeconomic order.

But Henry alone, Buell declares, gave this ambient enthusiasm memorable concrete embodiment in his essay "Civil Disobedience" and also (and especially) in *Walden*. "Thanks largely to their influence," Buell adds, "Emerson has become remembered as the prophet of self-reliance while Thoreau is the one who enacted it . . . The gusto with which *Walden* unpacks its ethics of self-sufficient simplicity and the work of house-building seems at once a robust response to [Emerson's] closing call in *Nature*, i.e., 'Build, therefore, your own world' and a reproach to its grandiosity. Indeed *Walden* stages the movement's most down-to-earth original enactment both of Emerson's vision of self-trust and of *Nature*'s multistep prescription for nature's awakening of a person's higher powers."

It seems then that both Henry's writings and his speaking engagements drove home, to whoever was willing to grab the golden ring, the *feeling* of transcendentalist concepts that his peers in this era sometimes struggled to communicate. Not to say that Henry communicated all he wished to convey perfectly every time and to every listener . . . but then again, who does?

His record probably landed with greater success than he himself even realized. His genuineness and his preference for stepping out of the writing bubble into the actual, fully dynamic real world, when it seemed time to do so, apparently made for both Henry and his fans all the difference.

BUSINESS LESSON

Let not to get a living be thy trade but thy sport. Is the business or career you're engaged in still fun? Was it ever? Are you enjoying marketing aspects, or do you wish you could bring someone else in to take something over? Henry is saying here to notice if your living feels like a "sport" versus a grinding "trade."

Your living, he maintains, should be enjoyable, fulfilling, and uplifting. If it's not, make some changes. If it is, go deeper into this good light and make it shine brighter.

Grab your favorite #2 and pencil in your business lesson here:

_____

_____

_____

12

CHILD'S PLAY

When any real progress is made,
we unlearn and learn anew what we thought we knew before.

mid his attempts to become a successful published writer,
Henry agreed in 1843 to tutor Ralph Waldo Emerson's nephew
Willie for one year in exchange for $100 room and board at Emerson's
brother William's home on Staten Island. This arrangement allowed
Henry to spend time knocking on doors in New York City so he could
meet with prominent editors and publishers, especially Horace
Greeley, publisher of the *New York Tribune*. A prominent national
figure who not only published Henry's work (and paid him for it) but
also enthusiastically functioned as his advocate and sometime literary agent, Greeley enjoyed finally meeting Henry in person and, as a
fan of Henry's work, began introducing him to other well-connected
publishing decision-makers in New York who might also agree to
help him get into print.

Similarly, Henry's side job as a tutor of Willie and caretaker
of Willie's kid brother and sister, enabled him to display that side
of him that his students back at the Concord Academy, as well as
Concord youngsters generally, loved about him. One who looked up
to him as the older brother she never had was eleven-year-old Louisa
May Alcott, who responded with great delight to his stories, essays,

nature walks, and creative bent in general. As a master of classical languages, Henry also reveled in mathematics, religion, philosophy, science, music (he so enjoyed pulling out his flute), and, well, learning itself. Thus, whatever price someone might agree to pay Henry to school and develop a young lad or lass could easily be termed a bargain by any measure.

Additionally, Henry had responded around this time to a Harvard alumni questionnaire asking about his professional occupation. He had a twofold response to this: schoolmaster, private tutor. As both consisted of "clients" who were children, taking care of students obviously felt most genuine to him at least for the time being, although it might also be a good guess that Henry chose these particular occupations because, at this point in his life, these seemed closest to a "real (paying) job" as opposed to a dream job within a long-term dream career. Those were still in process.

Henry for Kids

To introduce Henry to today's younger generation so they too might be positively affected by Henry's thinking, Corinne Hosfeld Smith, author of *Henry David Thoreau for Kids*, explains she created a special book format to help young readers "learn about Thoreau's contributions to our culture, and also get the chance to engage in hands-on projects that can bring Henry's ideas to life." She then adds, "It's the next best thing to Henry actually being there."

Corinne's book begins by chronicling Henry's varied contributions to the world around him, then coupling them with active assignments to show her readers how to follow in his footsteps. Many of the activities listed below are displayed on the book's back cover to ensure that its added value will not be missed:

- Building a model of Henry's cabin
- Keeping a daily journal just as Henry did

- Planting a garden (like the one Henry planted for Nathaniel and Sophia Hawthorne)
- Baking "trail-bread cakes"
- Going on a half-day hike
- Starting a rock collection

Beyond these assignments, *Henry David Thoreau for Kids* also lists resources, such as other books, websites, places to visit, and similar vehicles for connecting with Henry. While books *written* by Henry continue to thrive, the availability of a related workbook for *Walden* or other Henry titles wanes in comparison. To help with that, *Henry David Thoreau for Kids* attempts to fill this gap and keep youngsters today focused on Henry's values.

One potential companion to Corinne's book is a journaling version of Henry's *Walking* published by Applewood Books in Carlisle, Massachusetts, the rural town next door to Henry's hometown of Concord. Each page of this slim volume contains an excerpt from Henry's *Walking* such as these sample entries:

- *From the forest and wilderness come the tonics and barks which brace mankind.*
- *My desire to bathe my head in atmospheres unknown to my feet is perennial and constant.*
- *All good things are wild and free.*

The rest of the page is left free for diarists to fill however they wish: record their thoughts, compose a poem, sketch something, write a short (very short!) story, scribble, doodle . . . whatever comes to mind! Readers are thus able to share the same creative experiences that Henry allowed himself to enjoy in his own journaling.

The book *Build Your Castles in the Air* by Chuck Hansen, subtitled *Thoreau's Inspiring Advice for Success in Business (and Life) in the 21st Century*, includes a quotation from Henry at the top, under which the author adds a commentary of his own, often exploring how the quote relates to modern business and life. Categories of Henry quotations listed in the table of contents run the gamut from business to career to professional life, including:

- Finding your calling
- Managing your day-to-day work
- Managing your career
- Managing the business
- Managing your people
- Managing your working relationships (boss, coworkers, associates, vendors)
- Managing the business environment (society, government, culture)

Here are some of the Henry quotations included in this book:

- *We do not ride on the railroad, it rides upon us.*
- *Superfluous wealth can buy superfluities only.*
- *It is truly enough said that a corporation has no conscience, but a corporation of conscientious men is a corporation with a conscience.*

Viewing this through a modern business lens, one could easily position such books next to any number of contemporary workbooks that entrepreneurial thoughtleaders typically publish to serve as a marketing tool to educate readers to that entrepreneur-author's expertise, skill set, value propositions, and related strategies to be integrated into the reader's current business practices. Such a "practical guide" format assists the adoption of useful techniques that can drive the reader's own efforts toward business advancement and continued success.

Hikes, Boat Trips, and "Huckleberry Parties"

Henry's approach to life always found it easy, and desirable, to mix play with learning, whether sauntering around Walden Pond, huddled back in the classroom at his Concord Academy, while tutoring young Willie on Staten Island, or at a gathering in someone's Concord home, quite likely Orchard House, the home of the Alcotts.

Hard as this might be to believe, Henry at times could be the life of the party! Edward Waldo Emerson, son of Waldo and the founder of the Concord Museum, recalls countless hikes and boat trips and "huckleberry parties" where the "captain" (O my Henry!) of each berry-picking excursion would guide pickers to huckleberry locations.

On other occasions, maybe dinners and impromptu parties, Henry could spontaneously delight those present with clever poems and magic tricks or breaking out into a Scottish jig and joyful renditions of music merriment on his flute. More fun was had when Henry brought some corn for popping on such occasions. To Edward, as was the case for Louisa May, Henry was viewed as a lovable, fun older brother.

As regards nature in particular, Corinne confirms that Henry would invariably revert back to youngish behavior, stating: "Henry Thoreau had a childlike curiosity about the natural world. He could give full attention to even the smallest plant or flower. Today, kids have chances they rarely had back then, that is, to get this close to nature through programs at schools and local nature centers, and through 'No Child Left Inside' initiatives of environmental educators.

"Kids today are also more apt to question longstanding practices same as Henry used to," she adds. "Just because something is the way it's always been done, they might ask does this make it right? A young person will still have the capacity to wonder and won't just go along because everyone else is doing it. Adults: maybe yes, maybe no."

Thus Henry was always of a mind to do his best to remain childlike in a manner that is more in tune with current generations despite less encouragement for fresh thinking in Henry's day amid fewer resources. Henry could teach youth today a lot about how to involve themselves in the world around them, Corinne says, because they might be more open than the children—and adults!—of the mid-nineteenth century.

"The lesson of paying attention is something we really could use right now," she says. "Don't just stand around with your head down over some stupid screen. The natural world is full of interesting things." But when asked how Henry might respond to current events, she only chuckles.

"Politics? Climate change? He would probably just go for a walk."

For Henry, then, the answer, if you could find your way to it, may be that his approach begins with reducing materiality as much as possible so as to live as simply—and joyfully—as possible, and shunning as much as possible. In this way, Henry reasoned, we all might at least have a fighting chance of holding on to a child's spirit of play, discovery, adventure, and risk-taking. Those aspects of "adulthood" may be what many of us are most missing in our chase for business and personal "success."

FURTHER THOUGHTS
FROM HENRY ON CHILDREN

Children, who play life, discern its true law and relations more clearly than men, who fail to live it worthily, but who think that they are wiser by experience, that is, by failure.

I am convinced, both by faith and experience, that to maintain oneself on this earth is not a hardship but a pastime, if we will live simply and wisely.

As a mother loves to see her child imbibe nourishment and expand, so God loves to see his children thrive on the nutriment he has furnished them.

The senses of children are unprofaned. Their whole body is one sense—they take a physical pleasure in riding on a rail—they love to teeter—so does the unviolated—the unsophisticated mind derive an inexpressible pleasure from the simplest exercise of thoughts.

Rather than love, than money, than fame, give me truth.

BUSINESS LESSON

We should seek to be fellow students with the pupil, and should learn as well alongside him. Sometimes those we presume to teach are capable of teaching us right back. Be open to this, pay attention to what even your "inferior" pupil may have to contribute to you as well as you to him. The best atmosphere for learning, Henry would agree, is when everyone is learning together at the same pace.

Grab your favorite #2 and pencil in your business lesson here:

_____

_____

_____

13

THE HANDYMAN CAN!

Friends . . . they cherish one another's hopes.
They are kind to one another's dreams.

In 1847, when Waldo needed to find someone to help with chores around the house while he was away on a nine-month lecture tour of the UK, he immediately thought of Henry. But Henry was "away"—approaching the end of his second year at Walden Pond. Waldo likely assumed Henry would not be available, perhaps planning a third year at Walden rather than returning to Concord.

Like many people in town, Waldo knew Henry was the first to call for odd jobs: barn repairs, roof-raising, livestock care. Not only was Henry willing and skilled, he could frequently use the money as well. Name any task, and Henry had probably mastered it for someone in Concord.

Fortunately for Waldo, their timing aligned. As Waldo agonized over alternatives, Henry was wrestling with his own decision. As the crisp fall air of 1847 began to gather momentum, he knew he would have to choose between enduring another year of New England winter in his tiny house or packing things up and heading home. Ambling out of Walden Woods and onto the road to the village, he may have decided to head over to Waldo's farmhouse for advice. Waldo was always good for questions of that nature.

As Waldo's welcoming wife, Lidian, welcomed Henry at the door, he sensed opportunity. While Lidian fetched Waldo, Henry mused that Bush might be the answer to his dilemma. Perhaps he could move out of Walden and move in here!

"It would make all of us here at Bush so happy if you could take my place for a few months," Waldo blurted. "Unless of course you prefer to remain at Walden. But you're more than welcome to live and work on your writing here, and also help Lidian with chores and the children while I'm gone. For pay of course!"

Henry's mumbled response, later immortalized in *Walden*, betrayed his deliberation:

> *It seemed to me that I had several more lives to live, and could not spare any more time for that one.*

A few weeks later, Waldo waved goodbye to Henry and Lidian from the packet liner *Washington Irving* as it pulled out of Boston Harbor, reassured that his home and family were in good hands. Henry had agreed to stay until his return!

Later, back in Concord, Henry embraced his role as the Emersons' handyman, which meant handling a wide variety of challenges beyond simple groundskeeping:

Daily Chores
- Carpentry
- Bricklaying
- Masonry
- Gardening
- Painting
- Woodcutting
- Pruning
- Housecleaning
- Door/window repair

- Pet/livestock caretaking
- Fence repair
- Roof repair
- Grass/weed cutting

Caring for the Children

- Tutoring and helping with homework
- Playing games, including magic tricks
- Taking the children on nature excursions to Walden Pond and other local spots
- Skating and tobogganing in winter
- Boating and swimming in spring and summer down the Concord River
- Searching for arrowheads
- Assuring a child who falls that they will recover and be all right
- Fishing
- Reading or telling stories to help everyone fall asleep at night

Helping Lidian

- Lending an ear
- Occasionally helping in the kitchen
- Writing Waldo to give him updates of how things were going
- Lifting or moving heavy items in the house or barn
- Keeping things running smoothly
- Picking up supplies in the village and hauling them home

In return for room and board and a little remuneration, Henry was a veritable stand-in for Waldo. His appealing personality and mutual fondness for the Emersons made him one of the family. The children adored him—young Edward even asked Lidian if Henry could stay forever as a "second father." Lidian appreciated him as well and loved having him around.

Perhaps most important of all to Henry was that he even had time to write, maybe setting to his task in Waldo's favorite chair in the family library while Lidian and the children gave Henry sufficient space to think and write. This arrangement was in keeping with Waldo's role as Henry's mentor. Ever his guide and champion, Waldo ensured that writing time for Henry would be part of the bargain, equally important to the role as repairs and tutoring. Due to this understanding, the ten months Henry ended up spending with Waldo's family worked out well for everyone in every way.

BUSINESS LESSON

The most I can do for my friend is to simply be his friend. The best business relationships are those that feel like friendships. How do you feel when you get together with a client? Warm and safe or tense and fearful? Nurture the warm and safe ahead of all others. Refrain from encouraging those who make you tense and fearful. Life as a whole will be lived more happily this way.

Grab your favorite #2 and pencil in your business lesson here:

_____

_____

_____

14

HENRY'S DARK SIDE

What am I at present? A more miserable
object one could not well imagine.

G iven the wealth of reporting on the joy Henry imparted *to* children as well as joy imported *from* children, it would seem that Henry's day-to-day life, by and large, was one of great delight. It was challenging and frustrating, like all lives, but overall one can assume his was a happy, satisfying, centered life as he pursued his passions and lofty goals supported by friends, family, mentors, colleagues, neighbors and even, at times, intriguing strangers.

But life has a way of dragging even the most vibrant independent souls down to rock bottom at times. Henry was no exception, particularly in his twenties, a common age for confusion and emotional crises. These crossroads can conjure familiar questions:

- What do I really want in life?
- Who can help me figure this out?
- Why do I keep failing?
- Am I actually getting anywhere?
- Should I be trying something different?
- Do I offer society any value?

While such frustrations often resolve with age, Henry succumbed to their power just as painfully as any of the rest of us, though this period in his life is largely overlooked. As author and artist John Roman notes in the *Bangalore Review*, "A little-known dark side exists to Henry David Thoreau most historians avoid when describing the life of this notable literary figure."

Despite the generally positive depiction of Henry as "marching to the beat of a different drum," Roman writes that "Thoreau left behind over twenty years of extensive daily journals, and in those private reflections he confessed to frequent episodes of a depression so crippling that more than once brought him to the brink of suicide."

Not unlike many of us, Roman reports that Henry "had difficulties with self-esteem, personal relationships, social acceptance, and mood disorders," adding that "we've all seen upbeat, inspirational Thoreau quotes printed on a variety of products, but Henry's journals contain some shocking thoughts not likely to be considered for bumper stickers or t-shirts." An entry in his journal in 1843, for example, disclosed this surprising tidbit of cheerlessness: *What am I at present? A more miserable object one could not well imagine.*

And that wasn't all! In January of 1857, Henry brought his doomscrolling down a few clicks lower. *We are all ordinarily in a state of desperation; such is our life; oft-times it drives us to suicide.* Roman comments here: "Many disturbing comments [such as this] haunt the pages of Thoreau's journals."

Interestingly, most Thoreau scholarship ignores this darkness, focusing instead on his interests and achievements. Though occasionally a derogatory takedown appears to drag our hero through the mud—recall the slimy *New Yorker* "Pond Scum" article published in 2015—in general Henry's sense of balance and cheerful cynicism has kept him standing upright pretty well.

But Roman's commentary is a bit different from all that. In his case, a solid Henry supporter is reaching through a wall of sympathy to help us better understand him. One imagines that if Henry were still with us today, Roman might possibly be organizing an intervention to help our generous friend out of his sometimes dark wilderness (irony here!) fraught of mind and emotions.

To help us sort this all out further, Roman introduces American literary scholar Arnold Louis Weinstein to explain "how easy it is for us to look back and imagine Thoreau writing 'in peaceful solitude' at Walden Pond, [as] there is something deeply seductive about finding a 'free space' beyond culture." The truth, however, Roman interjects, is that Henry's "retreat" to Walden "was never intended to be a passive vacation. Thoreau clearly states in his book that he went to Walden, '. . . to transact some private business' and several historians now agree Henry's 'private business' was to separate himself from social distractions in order to resolve a serious despondency that was consuming him. In short, one of the main reasons Thoreau withdrew to the woods was to find a way to reconstruct his life."

Roman cites mental health experts who've diagnosed Henry posthumously with issues ranging from "severe bi-polar disorder, post-traumatic stress, mood swings, underlying depression, and struggles with his sexual orientation." But no matter, none other than Henry himself once weighed in on his troubles. In a January 1857 journal entry, Henry "self-diagnosed his own psychological imbalance," Roman writes, revealing: *My waking experience always has been, and is such, an alternate Rough and Smooth. In other words . . . it is Sanity and Insanity.*

"The point here is not to paint a negative picture of Thoreau," confides Roman, adding for balance's sake: "Actually, when Henry was on the upside of his manic-depressive temperament he displayed an astounding sense of optimism and wisdom, an aspect of his writing that has always resonated with readers."

And to "brighten the analysis further," Roman quotes Dr. Michael Sperber, author of the book *Henry David Thoreau: Cycles and Psyche*: "Despite the mental afflictions Thoreau suffered beginning in childhood, he maintained a positive attitude. Although Thoreau was severely depressed at times, it was never for long. Thoreau was challenge-oriented. Whatever did not destroy him, he believed, would contribute to his strengths."

"Wake Up to Who You Are"

Did Henry ever resolve his issues? Roman believes he did, noting that the years 1840 to 1847, when Henry was twenty-three to thirty, were "pivotal in his psychic salvation." Though he was continually feeling in a "state of deterioration," none other than Waldo came to his rescue. Fourteen years older, Waldo took Henry on as a protégé, mentoring him, opening doors to his vast connections, and serving as a writing—and, frankly—life coach.

Perhaps most significant of all, Waldo was the one who suggested to Henry, not long after Henry's graduation from Harvard, that he start keeping a daily journal. Acting upon that suggestion only a few hours later, Henry began his journal and never stopped, adding to it nearly every evening for over twenty years. Journal writing, Roman writes, "gave Henry an early glimpse of his special talent for self-expression and introduced him to the powers writing held for releasing feelings." His journals would total two million words and were published posthumously.

Today we know from contemporary psychology that journaling *does* work to counteract depression. And from what we know of what it did for Henry, it apparently worked very, very well. For one thing, it awakened in him an understanding of the work that he needed to do all by himself. This pushed him off the precipice of depression into the cool, calming waters of self-acceptance. How else to account for his grouping of these enlightened exhortations:

> *Wake up to who you are and to what really matters in life. Our true reform can be undertaken any morning before unbarring our doors. Only that day dawns to which we are awake.*

Because of all this, Roman concludes his analysis with this second benefit from journaling: "Henry was hooked. He poured himself into his writing and found it eased his mental blocks and opened him up to life. Whatever troubled Henry on any given day was exorcised from his emotional life and exiled to the written word. The tactic worked so well that Thoreau became hyper-graphic for the remainder of his life."

NOTE: John Roman is a regular contributor to *Artists Magazine* and has written for several other national art publications as well as *The Concord Saunterer*. In 2024, visitors to Thoreau Farm got a close look at the fifteen places Henry lived in his hometown of Concord, Massachusetts, via an exhibit of Roman's historically accurate pen-and-ink renderings. Several of these drawings appeared in *Electrum Magazine* alongside his essay "The Homes of Henry David Thoreau."

BUSINESS LESSON

The mass of men lead lives of quiet desperation . . . and go to the grave with a song still in them. Henry did not actually say the second portion of this quotation, although many have attributed it to him. But its suggestion is a good one: Sing your song *now*, sing it *loud*, sing it *for all to hear*. Don't wait until you have no more time to sing it at all. People around you, in business or at home with your family, will appreciate you for it and feel safe enough to sing their own songs too.

Grab your favorite #2 and pencil in your business lesson here:

_____

_____

_____

15

HENRY THE SUCCESSFUL AUTHOR!

Write while the heat is in you.

By 1843, Waldo and *New York Tribune* editor-publisher Horace Greeley had both come to view Henry as a fast-rising star. Both these luminaries had even committed to unearthing whatever opportunities they could find for him, spending a lot of time and personal capital calling in favors and touting this young unknown from Massachusetts to their literary contacts. Greeley was convinced that Henry would be an asset to any publication or book publisher, given his natural talent and innovative point of view.

Waldo went so far as to arrange for Henry a means of living and working in the New York City area rent-free at the Staten Island home of his brother William, an attorney and judge in Manhattan. Henry could also earn an additional $100, it was decided, if he stayed a full year and tutored William's young son Willie. Henry, as we know, loved children and had proven himself a master teacher and tutor, yet his main motivation for accepting this position was to give himself time to write while developing opportunities to write for money.

Henry's New York Adventure

At first this arrangement seemed perfect and Henry looked forward to taking advantage of Greeley's and Waldo's connections to see where they'd lead him. It seemed a great place to start given that both friends had done much to get him published thus far. When Greeley read Henry's profile of Thomas Carlyle, for example, he chose right then and there to publish it in the *Tribune*. And Waldo, staying in constant touch with Henry by letter, repeatedly invited him—begged him, even!—to write something for *The Dial* even while traversing New York. Henry, however, based now in a metropolis so far from his hometown, was increasingly turning his sights toward other targets on the Manhattan horizon.

An early victory in this regard, though one that had at first appeared a potentially stunning defeat, centered on an essay commissioned by John O'Sullivan, editor of New York's *Democratic Review*, a connection of Nathaniel Hawthorne's. The assignment was that Henry review a book by John Adolphus Etzler, a German engineer and inventor who emigrated to the United States in 1831 with a vision of creating a technical utopia. His new book was an enthusiastic account of emerging technological advances of the time, predicting that the world was on its way to become grander and more astonishing than ever. Though usually curious about new machines and inventions, Henry's review of the book was fraught with barbs puncturing much of what Etzler had to say.

Though his treatment of the Etzler book probably offered *Democratic Review* subscribers a juicy read—and a potential controversy that might lead to more magazine sales—O'Sullivan had a different reaction. A gleeful follower of Etzler and his prophecies, O'Sullivan disdained Henry's review and rejected his piece out of hand. But he could not dismiss that Henry had nonetheless written a "lively and pointed essay." As a result O'Sullivan suggested he might still be willing to publish the review if Henry toned down his ferocity. If perhaps Henry could do a little "modifying and adjusting," the piece would be more palatable to readers who sympathized with and/or outright approved of Etzler's vision.

One might imagine that, given his goal of breaking into the New York literary market, Henry might be amenable to this compromise. The *Democratic Review*, Henry knew, reached a much larger audience than he had ever enjoyed before, so why not take O'Sullivan's deal? But, according to biographer Laura Dassow Walls: "Henry would not back down."

It is easy to recall similar stories throughout history about an unknown wannabee, desperately striving to make a name for themselves, gambling on their own talent and capabilities by holding out for what *they* felt was the best way rather than giving in to the so-called experts or powers that be. One example from recent memory, from the world of motion pictures, involved a standoff in the mid-1970s . . .

A Chance to Lose Everything

In the early 1970s, Sylvester Stallone, at the time an unknown and literally penniless actor/screenwriter submitted a draft of his first *Rocky* film to numerous film studios and was rejected by every studio but one. Universal Pictures, the last studio left standing, made Stallone an offer that its studio heads felt certain he would not, and could not, refuse.

Their offer was $100,000 for the script in return for *all* rights and *all* decisions regarding the production of the film. That would include, of course, who would play Rocky himself, a character Stallone felt only he could play. Meanwhile, at the top of Universal's list were such contemporary megastars as Burt Reynolds, Robert Redford, Ryan O'Neal, and James Caan.

But Stallone, by his own admission a "complete nobody," insisted that only *he,* despite being unknown, could play the title character. Only *he* knew the right way to play Rocky. Stallone also believed, he revealed later, that if he could pull such a portrayal off, it would surely bestow stardom on himself and blockbuster success to the film.

The veteran Universal producers thought he was crazy, but Stallone wouldn't budge, even in the face of the producers upping their offer to $300,000. Since the producers recognized the script's potential, they greenlighted Stallone to play the lead with the proviso that his up-front cash payment would be only $35,000.

Had Stallone been wrong about his ability to play this title character, we would not be talking about him today. But "Yo, Adrian, he did it!" and eventually, because Hollywood deals typically include box office "points" (i.e., percentages), Stallone earned $2,500,000 from points plus a *Rocky II* sequel and a greenlight for other scripts he had written previously (but had never been able to sell) . . . and whatever else Stallone wanted to do. Summing it all up to Johnny Carson one night on the *Tonight Show*, he cracked: "They'd make a movie of my parking tickets if I let them."

Henry then was cut from the same cloth as risk-takers like Stallone (or was it the other way around?), willing to take a chance at losing *everything* should their faith in themselves be overblown. Though such an attitude can sometimes succeed, such as when Horace Greeley reacted enthusiastically to Henry's profile of Carlyle and purchased it on the spot, other risks can result in big misses like a New York editor outright dismissing him and only perfunctorily wishing him well. Not everyone, you see, is gonna "get it."

Of course, in between the actual assignments and opportunities, Henry frequently filled the time, as most entrepreneurs and professionals will do, with what we now call networking or, "just getting out and around to meet people," especially those that Waldo, Hawthorne, Greeley, and others recommended as liable to lead to great business opportunities.

Henry T. Meets Henry J.

One such early business encounter in Henry's New York adventure was a visit to the home of theologian Henry James Sr. in Washington Square. This experience buoyed Henry's hopes that good things were bound to happen.

Though it couldn't be known at the time that James's little children would all grow up to be successful in various intellectual circles—Henry Jr. as a renowned novelist, William James as a well-known philosopher and psychologist, Alice James whose diary was published posthumously to great acclaim—the visit with Henry Sr. struck Henry T. as a very positive and enjoyable experience. Perhaps, if all went well, Henry surmised, an ongoing relationship such as this one would not only be good for Henry's business/writing prospects but for his mental and emotional frame of mind as well.

Henry's evaluation, written out after the three-hour get-together, went this way: *I have been to see Henry James and like him very much . . . He is a refreshing, forward looking, and forward moving, man [who] has naturalized and humanized New York for me.* This sort of "spring in your step" is of the sort that we all need from time to time to balance out tensions and anxieties from attempting to climb up the business/career ladder. Regardless of whether such a get-together ever leads to a genuine, useful opportunity, which in fact this one never did, it can be a healthy experience that enables one to continue moving forward, and in good spirits.

So the bounce it gave Henry, as a defense against his dismay at the very look and feel of New York City, proved bolstering. Too much of his time was spent in what we now call the Big Apple, a long, slender island packed with wall-to-wall buildings all within a few feet or narrow alleyway of each other. There were no sanctuaries, little or big, no breathing areas like playgrounds, gardens, benches for settling down in the fresh air to rest a bit. Central Park would not be created until 1858—fifteen more years!

This likely had Henry asking himself, *Where were the woodlands? Where are the many varieties of birds? Where can one find some flowers? Where are the badgers and beavers and deer? Where is the solace?* Staten Island had some of this (i.e., solitude), but even that, given where Henry hailed from, was lacking.

Then came a second networking encounter, writes Laura Dassow Walls, when Henry dropped in on his tutor Henry McKean (yet *another* Henry!) from back in his Harvard days, this time at the Mercantile Association Library where McKean's position was such that he was able to grant Henry full access to the library's reading room, at no charge. This led to introductions "right on the library's steps," as Walls phrases it, with famed utopian reformers Henry Wright, Albert Brisbane, and William Henry Channing. Now Henry was mingling within a wholly robust world of New York thoughtleaders, which elevated him from the parochial bubble of the village of Concord and prodded him to keep at his attempts to build bridges to success.

Ultimately, however, it wasn't enough. In the weeks following, there came a point when Henry decided he'd been beating his head against the wall in this unfamiliar metropolis, pushing himself down the mobbed, dirty, and loud New York streets and too frequently meeting only rejection at the hands of leading publications like *The Knickerbocker* and those founded by the Harper brothers.

"So sorry, we'd really like to bring your work into our pages, but unfortunately we just do not have the budget to do so. We wish you luck though." Gasp. *My, how some things never change*, Henry must have thought! No one ever has "the budget to do so."

Such editing clashes and dark moments invariably arose at the expense of Henry's attempts to say exactly what he meant and to express exactly how he felt. This dynamic fuels the typical personality of many a "true writer" whose writing decisions must not be taken lightly nor attended to in a way that leaves the writer reeling at an unwelcome surprise editorial change or two . . . or more! For Henry, after many months of these surprises, it was time to close up his New York shop.

If this frustrating May to December effort was a signal, however, that success so far from Concord was not to be, Henry rather quickly settled into his Plan B, which was to return to Concord and accept his fate, not as a sad failure returning home with his tail between his legs but rather as an uplifting commitment to achieve what he had always wanted to attain in the first place, and in a locale where he might achieve it entirely on his own terms: his hometown of Concord. His self-judgment then was summed up by this succinct observation, that his New York adventure, though a personal defeat, could also be termed *heaven's success.*

Why was "making it" in New York City the only true definition of "making it"? Why couldn't his return to Concord constitute a much *more* exciting opportunity and a second chance to embrace Concord as the seat of his eventual true and lasting triumph? He had, after all, been known to say, *How lucky was I to have been born in the most estimable place in the world and just in the nick of time, etc.* Perhaps focusing on Concord and all that Concord contained and offered would more likely lead him where he wanted to go. New York may in fact have been the very opposite of what he needed to do and where he needed to do it from.

So let us go home!

Book #1: *A Week on the Concord and Merrimack Rivers*

By the time Henry's brother, John, died of lockjaw on January 11, 1842, Henry had already closed up their school. When he'd finished building his cabin at Walden and had moved himself into it, he knew he faced a major and meaningful decision: what to write about in his new personal world of "living deliberately." He could address many topics of great interest to him—nature, solitude, humanity, writing, philosophy, slavery—but in the end, one topic he just couldn't shake was a need to remember his beloved brother and render some kind of tribute that would keep John's spirit alive.

But how and what? A biography of John perhaps? A memoir of his life with John? A listing of all John's achievements? None of these approaches seemed quite right, but *something* had to be done.

What ultimately emerged instead was an account of a trip that he and John had taken in 1839 in a well-outfitted rowboat that shoved off initially along the Concord River and continued downriver until they reached the deeper Merrimack River at Lowell, Massachusetts. From there, they rowed up the Merrimack to Hooksett Pinnacle, north of Bedford, New Hampshire—over fifty miles from where they'd begun. After stowing their boat, they took to the roads, walking, taking a stagecoach, and walking again all the way to the top of Mount Washington—a good eighty miles farther.

Like the trip itself, writing such an account likely struck Henry as beyond daunting. How to pull this off, he must have wondered, how much to write, what specifics to include, how to describe John, how to describe his emotional attachment to John. Above all, how to depict such an endeavor that, at many moments, could easily be remembered as mundane while at other moments the air was bright with exhilaration and discovery. And even more, how to enliven this account as a glowing portrait of John stimulating enough to capture and maintain his readers' attention.

These were big challenges, the writer in Henry knew, though no more so than what any other writer faced at any level of their career. In Henry's case, his "level" ranked, he felt, at nearly the bottom rung of his writing ladder. Not the very bottom maybe but not far above it.

At this point in his career, for example, he had published only a handful of poems and essays, chiefly by Margaret Fuller, editor of *The Dial*, who alongside her decision to accept Henry's work came difficult feedback indicating that he had much more to learn despite an obvious talent for prose. Little by little, despite rejecting Henry's submissions here and there, she grew more openly encouraging of Henry and noted him as an up-and-coming "someone to watch." But she remained a tough tasker nonetheless, preventing Henry from viewing himself as having quite yet "made it" in the writing world.

What's more, this time Henry's challenge seemed more formidable than ever. He could see the rung where this, his first *book,* laid in wait for him, but he couldn't reach up and grab it. If he was finally feeling more confident about his poems, essays, other short pieces, this time he had nothing to fall back on. How *long*, for example, should his book be? Where should he begin his account? How should it end? And what to put in the middle of all that?

His many questions were disconcerting and disruptive. And only he could figure out the answers.

Flash forward to the end of Henry's first year in his Walden cabin. He had by now transformed into a hard-driving writer who was deep in his flow, hacking diligently away at his manuscript day in and day out, concentration broken only slightly now and then by birds singing gaily in nearby trees or by the daily visit of the fidgety squirrel who lived nearby, here to scoop bread crumbs from the cabin floor. Thus pushing on, Henry had found a writing rhythm that could answer all his questions, the biggest one his raison d'être: to manifest his goal to "*live life deliberately*" by elucidating his brother's memory for all who wished to behold it.

The result was *A Week on the Concord and Merrimack Rivers* with the intended scope a sort of travelogue-adventure-memoir with Henry and John as two young protagonists paddling down these New England rivers in the direction of, but not actually reaching, their mouth at the Atlantic Ocean. In addition, much of the book's text also deviated in places that allowed extended observations from Henry, including judgments, mini-lectures, and musings, that, for many readers, amounted to a wondrous illustration of Henry-as-philosopher rather than merely Henry-as-adventurer.

For those who found such diversions provocative or entertaining, all was copacetic. But for other readers, wandering so deeply into digressions from the expected plotline felt too much like rambling. Thus those who wanted the book to hew closer to what the title suggested found the book's meanderings annoying, unhelpful, or even boring.

The first paragraph of course attests to set the tone. A reader's personal reaction may determine in which direction they would want the rest of the book text to go. Consider your own reaction as you read this initial passage:

> *The Musketaquid, or Ground-grass River, though probably as old as the Nile or the Euphrates, did not begin to have a place in civilized history until the fame of its grassy meadows and its fish attracted settlers out of England in 1635, when it received the other but kindred name of Concord from the first plantation on its banks, which appears to have been commenced in a spirit of peace and harmony. It will be Ground-grass River as long as grass grows and water runs here; it will be Concord River only while men lead peaceable lives on its banks.*

Now consider the differences of the following reviews:

Bronson Alcott sat right down on the day he received his copy and read it straight through in forty-eight hours. His verdict: "An American book, worthy to stand by Emerson's Essays on my shelves."

George Ripley, in contrast, gave *A Week* a somewhat different evaluation, posting a scathing review on the front page of the *New York Tribune* brandished with adjectives such as "execrable, dubious, dangerous, a revolting attack on good sense and good taste" . . . you get the idea!

James Russell Lowell, taking a middle road, was less scornful in his *Massachusetts Quarterly Review*, praising much of the book for its descriptions, especially of nature along the way. But despite this positive appraisal, Lowell also criticized other aspects of the book as "self-indulgent and lacking in originality." Then, to make matters worse, Lowell labeled Henry a Waldo "imitator with an inflated sense of self-importance." Suggesting Henry was a poor carbon copy of the so-called Sage of Concord (Waldo) was surely the last thing Henry wanted to read!

The result of this "split decision" from reviewers had to have affected the book's word-of-mouth. As is true today, a book's success has everything to do with its reader reactions. When converted into recommendations to potential readers—friends, family, colleagues, blog followers, readers of book reviews, TikTok followers!—reactions will land as some form of "You *must* read this, it is *terrific!*" or "Well, it didn't do much for me, it left me cold." Whether they're reporting on a movie, book, or TV show, how much we trust the individual giving the review heavily influences whether we plunk our money down or pass on the experience. In Henry's day, this was no less true.

Consequently, Henry's first book failed to sell more than a couple hundred copies. In today's era of print-on-demand technology, a publisher or author need not print out any more books than actually get purchased. In Henry's time, the reality of book publishing was very different. Back then, and in some cases in our present era as well, a publisher will arrange with a printer to print, let's say, three thousand copies of a new book in the expectation—or is it *hope?*—of the book "doing well" and selling all three thousand, followed by another "print run" of perhaps an additional few thousand (or more).

In Henry's case, "fortunately," the number was lower than most, to the tune of just over nine hundred copies. I put quotation marks around *fortunately* because although this lower number saved him from a total financial disaster, it in fact did not save him very much. This owes to the fact that Henry's "publisher" James Munroe had negotiated an arrangement with Henry that if any copies of his book failed to sell, Henry would be on the hook for purchasing the remaining copies. This sort of arrangement differs little, if at all, from today's so-called self-publishing or hybrid publishing arrangements, which is to suggest that Henry's first book was never published by a true publisher at all!

For Henry then, whose *A Week* ended up only selling 200 or so copies with 706 unsold books the most common historical reference. In any case, 700+ unsold obviously represented a significant financial hit. Yet after a year or two, Munroe insisted on calling in this debt and dumping the 700+ copies in Henry's lap. Henry, however, literally did not have the means to remit the balance of Munroe's invoice, so Munroe agreed to be paid in installments, which meant Henry sent

Munroe a payment whenever he could gather the money to do so. This ended up taking Henry about four years to pay off.

To his credit, Henry kept his sense of humor about this outcome to the extent that he could. When friends would come over to visit him in his apartment, they would often marvel at all the many, many books on his bookshelves. "Oh, so many books!" they might cry, "how impressive!" To which Henry would invariably respond: "Yes, I have nine hundred volumes there . . . seven hundred of which I have written myself!"

Book #2: *Walden; or, Life in the Woods*

It would be seven drafts and nine years before Henry's second book, *Walden; or, Life in the Woods* was published. This time, it can be assumed, Henry would have two distinctly different objectives for this second book that he lacked the first time around:

1. This time land a "real" publisher as opposed to a *printer* like James Munroe. Locking his stock of *A Week* in a closet and taking them out only when someone came looking to buy, Munroe needn't carry out any extraneous effort—like publicity!—to promote Henry's book. Instead he had merely to count the number of books sold and charge authors accordingly as per their contract for all unsold copies.

An authentic publisher in those days would instead at least *attempt* to help an author sell books, one way or another. Then, if such efforts were fruitless, the publisher would swallow the cost of printing the books, and that would be that.

2. Work harder on the manuscript and seek feedback so that the final product could be as great as possible. Looking back, it seemed from its reviews that *A Week* suffered badly from Henry's digressions, a problem that Henry might have dealt with if he had gotten some advice to that effect from, for example, Waldo and maybe

Margaret Fuller, Horace Greeley, and other supportive literary professionals. This time he would incorporate such colleagues' advice.

The result of this was *Walden; or, Life in the Woods*, a manuscript seven drafts and nine years in the making, published in 1854. But the proof is in the pudding, or in the case of book publishing, brisk sales derive from tasty reviews. Most were lavish in their praise.

Accolades tumbled in from every corner, especially from peers. He gifted a copy to Bronson Alcott a few days after publication and was ecstatic twenty-four hours later when Alcott informed him that the day before he had read the whole thing and that now, one day later, he had read it through a second time! Alcott's verbiage, as was true with his reaction to *A Week*, was effusive.

Next, George Eliot, in a review for *The Westminster Review*, praised *Walden* for capturing "a bit of pure American life" and for its "energetic, yet calm spirit of innovation."

Then Waldo too joined the chorus: "All American kind are delighted with *Walden* as far as they have dared to say."

Nathaniel Hawthorne chimed as well although privately, in his journal, praising Henry for his singular gift for observation, extolling him as a "keen and delicate observer of nature" and a "genuine" observer overall.

And poet John Greenleaf Whittier also complimented Henry on the book, although criticizing its message (jokingly it seemed) that man should lower himself to the level of a woodchuck and walk on four legs. Nonetheless he raved that "Thoreau's *Walden* is a capital reading," then adding a second joke that "(but) for me, I prefer walking on two legs."

Following the reviews, *Walden* was indeed a hit, although a slowly awakening one, selling only 1,700 copies in its first year. This was therefore not really a commercial hit but an artistic success for sure. Commercially, despite all this attention and publicity, *Walden* in fact went out of print once the full allotment of 2,000 was sold out in 1859. Interest in it persisted, however, and in 1862—the year of Henry's death—*Walden* was republished. From that point on, its popularity grew steadily, ensuring it would never go out of print again.

Over the following decades, glowing reviews from America's foremost literary voices gradually propelled *Walden* to bestseller status. Today it stands as a perennial favorite—cherished by individual readers, studied in classrooms, and discussed in book clubs. What began as a modest publication has ultimately earned its place as a celebrated classic of American literature.

Acclaimed novelist John Updike, writing with a touch of humor in the mid-twentieth century, lauded *Walden* this way: "A century and a half after its publication, *Walden* has become such a totem of the back-to-nature, preservationist, anti-business, civil-disobedience mindset, and Thoreau so vivid a protester, so perfect a crank and hermit saint, that the book risks being as revered and unread as the Bible."

The American psychologist B. F. Skinner allowed that he carried a copy of *Walden* with him throughout his youth, eventually inspiring him to compose, in 1945, *Walden Two*, about a fictional utopia where people attempt to live together in harmony under the sway of Henry's ideals.

Robert Frost even put a capper on the *Walden* phenomenon with a short but to-the-point message declaring: "In one book . . . [Thoreau] surpasses everything we have had in America."

Meanwhile, back at *Walden*'s earliest incarnation, Henry's publisher—yes, this time an authentic one—Ticknor and Fields, though better known (then and today) as the Old Corner Bookstore in the heart of downtown Boston, beamed with ecstasy. Its top brass applauded themselves for persuading Henry to join their impressive growing author roster that would ultimately also embrace the likes of Henry Wadsworth Longfellow, Harriet Beecher Stowe, Mark Twain, Henry James, and Henry's Concord cohorts Hawthorne and Waldo.

Given *Walden*'s growing acclaim, this second book confirmed he'd been on the right track all along. Rather than forging success by pounding the hard, cold pavement of New York, Henry's triumph achieved from his solitary life on the shores of Walden Pond likely felt to Henry so much more fulfilling. Ironically, the commercial failure of *A Week* may have been essential—granting Henry the unhurried time needed to refine *Walden* into something extraordinary.

As Thoreau scholar Robert Sayre noted, *Walden* "uses material not just from 1845–47 but down to 1854. Thus in *Walden*, social criticism, autobiography, moral philosophy, and natural history are all integrated, making a book with many different facets and themes but which most readers find brilliantly unified."

Transcendental scholar Lawrence Buell agrees with this, adding that "both readers and publishers come into play in the process of a book becoming a 'classic' and this is especially true of *Walden*, which was commended by generations of presumably qualified readers whose opinions carry enough weight to perpetuate themselves." On the flip side, Buell explains that such opinions must wend their way through the literary marketplace "and be sustained by a series of successful publishing ventures, which in themselves can affect readerly opinion. [In other words] the influence is mutual, not one-way."

In 1903, he continues, George H. Mifflin, the president of *Walden*'s newest publisher, Houghton Mifflin, declared that "'Thoreau should be our next great author after Emerson.' This decision inaugurated the 1906 20-volume edition of Thoreau's collected writings, a historic publishing event commonly taken as the point of Thoreau's canonization." But this was no "publisher conspiracy" that finally drove Henry's popularity, Buell reminds us. In fact, "an historic would be fairer to surmise that despite Houghton Mifflin's backing he almost didn't make it. Before 1880, no book by Thoreau achieved an average sale of more than 200 copies annually; in the 1890s, the firm sold only 310 copies of its first edition of Thoreau's collected works, the ten-volume Riverside edition; and the 1906 edition was not reprinted for decades."

"Thoreau has had many disciples and people who preached his cause," Buell writes, although "no one would have listened to them if our culture wasn't ready to hear what he had to say. The inchoate complex of social habits and attitudes we call 'culture' was reorienting itself toward the end of the nineteenth century in such a way as to benefit Thoreau [whose] status as the father of a genre of 'out-of-door' literature is being noted to his credit rather than as a sign of minor status. This assessment reflects the increase in production, sales, and critical praise of nonfictional nature writing in America . . . (and the) rise of preservationist, and more broadly, anti-industrialist sentiment."

Buell concludes by quoting Harding, who once stated, simply: "[Henry's] book has never been out of print since then."

BUSINESS LESSON

I learned this, at least, by my experiment; that if one advances confidently in the direction of his dreams, and endeavors to live the life which he has imagined, he will meet with a success unexpected in common hours. If Henry says he learned this, we have to believe him! Try experimenting with your own imagined life and see what happens. Happy you will be if your outcome is the same as Henry's!

Grab your favorite #2 and pencil in your business lesson here:

_____

_____

_____

_____

_____

16

TRAVELS WITH HENRY

Simply to see to a distant horizon through a clear air—
the fine outline of a distant hill or a blue mountaintop
through some new vista—this is wealth enough
for one afternoon.

Henry once wrote: *I have traveled a great deal . . . right here in Concord!* And travel he did, all up and over Concord's hills, down the roads and streets, in bare feet along the shores of not only Walden Pond but the other ponds in the area too (White Pond, Sandy Pond, Warner's Pond, and more), through farms, hinterlands, grassy meadows, and private estates.

As well, in the environs amid both waterways and the driest grounds, there stood, of course, trees, trees, and more trees. Walden Pond is especially famous for its surrounding forest, Walden Woods, just as other landmarks gain character from theirs: Lincoln Woods, Wyman's Meadow, Ice Fort Cove, Goose Pond, and Pheasant Hill, with its bewitching perfect view of Wachusett Mountain thirty-five miles away.

Henry referred to these travels as *sauntering*, which he explained this way:

I have met with but one or two persons in the course of my life who understood the art of Walking, that is, of taking walks—who had a genius, so to speak, for sauntering, which word is beautifully derived "from idle people who roved about the country, in the Middle Ages, and asked charity, under pretense of going a la Sainte Terre," to the Holy Land, till the children exclaimed, "There goes a Sainte-Terrer," a Saunterer, a Holy-Lander. They who never go to the Holy Land in their walks, as they pretend, are indeed mere idlers and vagabonds; but they who do go there are saunterers in the good sense, such as I mean . . . [For] every walk is a sort of crusade, preached by some Peter the hermit in us, to go forth and reconquer this Holy Land from the hands of the Infidels.

So he wasn't just jogging through field and stream nor mindlessly ambling along. He insisted that walking worked best when one had a worthwhile destination in mind—an actual *crusade!*—a raison d'être and an intention to ensure that your every walk would lead to something momentous.

He would never have fit our modern idea of walking—what President Harry Truman called his "daily constitutional": a leisurely stroll around a block or two for fresh air, perhaps idly chitchatting or gossiping along the way with a companion . . . but not much else.

Although, if we might speculate, we might wonder if Henry would see value in today's marathons and 5K races. After all, they offer an "end game"—a crusade of sorts. The weeks or months of training culminate in that moment: lining up, taking a deep breath, awaiting the official holler—"Runners . . . GO!"—and then surging forward with hundreds (or thousands) of others.

For many years—until the Covid lockdown put an end to it—a five-mile road race took place every Fourth of July right in the heart of Concord, its starting line just down the street from the Concord Free Public Library and thus not far from the now long-gone Thoreau "Texas House." I used to run in this race myself, joyfully, every year, breezing past Concord's famous 1716 Colonial Inn (where Henry's family briefly lived), then pounding over the Old North Bridge before circling back past where the town center's prominent grist mill building (now a busy restaurant) stands, and then pushing myself that final mile to the finish line alongside Emerson Field.

If Henry were still with us, would we have run together? Perhaps we would have chatted at the starting line, then leapt forward at the *crack-crack* of two minuteman-clad officials firing muskets to signal our start. Mayhaps, who knows?

Or maybe Henry would just stand on the side of the road shaking his head and muttering, "What fools these Concordians be?" before sauntering off toward Walden Pond for his usual four-hour exploration of its woods. Who can say?

Blossoms, Hawks, Noisy Toads

Whatever he might have thought regarding road racing today, we know that Henry took pride in telling farmer clients—especially during his surveying projects—that he already knew their land intimately. Whether behind the barn, or in a grove of apple trees past the cow pasture, along a path rarely taken (to paraphrase Robert Frost!), or on an Indian trail like the one that led to Egg Rock—the site of the first indigenous peoples camp thousands of years before—his familiarity with the land was unmatched.

"I know your land better than you do!" he often remarked, to a landowner's chagrin. Not many Concordians could utter such a boast!

And like many things about Henry, this sauntering has inspired growing bands of fans to emulate him, wandering their own hometowns, proud to spread this noble habit—alone or in self-appointed "sauntering societies."

They gather in groups of five, six, or even a dozen, some wearing Thoreau Society T-shirts (I SAUNTERED IN WALDEN WOODS) stenciled on their backs, others in Henry's signature straw hat or a flannel shirt and L.L.Bean boots perfect for cooler weather or muddy trails.

The glory of sauntering is its flexible pace, which encourages one to shift gears, slow down, and indulge their curiosity. For instance:

- Are those early spring flower blossoms sprouting at my feet?
- Look! A red-winged hawk perched on a tree branch just above our heads!
- Shhh . . . Listen to that chorale of noisy toads belching loudly over by that swampland.

So much of what attracted Henry and caused him to gasp in delight were pleasant surprises one could notice only by slowing down. This remains a major benefit of sauntering and is a vital skill for certain careers or enterprises such as explorers, adventurers, travel guides . . . or travel writers!

Henry Beyond Concord's Borders

Despite that famed quip about doing so much traveling *right here in Concord*, the truth of it all was that Henry also journeyed many miles *beyond* Concord and its borders throughout much of his adult life. Although most of his writing chronicling these excursions was buried in his posthumously published journals or essays, they ultimately were published in book form. Consider these titles: *Cape Cod*, *The Maine Woods*, *A Yankee in Canada* . . . even *Walking!*

Other travelogues that never happened (but might have!) could have covered his explorations of Minnesota, New Jersey, New York City, Fire Island, Lake Champlain in Vermont, New Hampshire, Cohasset (Massachusetts), and Mount Katahdin in Maine.

Yes, indeed, just as he had said, Henry had traveled a great deal—and he had written about his traveling a great deal as well! As he often took notes while exploring new worlds, some of his writings met with great acclaim from his steadily expanding circle of fans.

Had there been a travel writer position open at the *Boston Evening Traveller* or the *New York Tribune*, Henry's travels, such as those found in *The Maine Woods*, *Cape Cod*, and *Walking* might well have marked him as the Rick Steves of his day.

Enjoy these samples:

Cape Cod
by Henry D. Thoreau

We had forgotten how far a stage could go in a day, but we were told that the Cape roads were very "heavy," though they added that, being of sand, the rain would improve them. This coach was an exceedingly narrow one, but as there was a slight spherical excess over two on a seat, the driver waited till nine passengers had got in, without taking the measure of any of them, and then shut the door after two or three ineffectual slams, as if the fault were all in the hinges or the latch,— while we timed our inspirations and expirations so as to assist him.

We were now fairly on the Cape, which extends from Sandwich eastward thirty-five miles, and thence north and northwest thirty more, in all sixty-five, and has an average breadth of about five miles. In the interior it rises to the height of two hundred, and sometimes perhaps three hundred feet above the level of the sea. According to Hitchcock, the geologist of the State, it is composed almost entirely of sand, even to the depth of three hundred feet in some places, though there is probably a concealed core of rock a little beneath the surface, and it is of diluvian origin, excepting a small portion at the extremity and elsewhere along the shores, which is alluvial.

For the first half of the Cape large blocks of stone are found, here and there, mixed with the sand, but for the last thirty miles boulders, or even gravel, are rarely met with. Hitchcock conjectures that the ocean has, in course of time, eaten out Boston Harbor and other bays in the mainland, and that the minute fragments have been deposited by the currents at a distance from the shore, and formed this sand-bank. Above the sand, if the surface is subjected to agricultural tests, there is found to be a thin layer of soil gradually diminishing from Barnstable to Truro, where it ceases; but there are many holes and rents in this weather-beaten garment not likely to be stitched in time, which reveal the naked flesh of the Cape, and its extremity is completely bare.

The Maine Woods
by Henry D. Thoreau
Ktaadn

On the 31st of August 1846, I left Concord in Massachusetts for Bangor and the backwoods of Maine, by way of the railroad and steamboat, intending to accompany a relative of mine engaged in the lumber-trade in Bangor, as far as a dam on the west branch of the Penobscot, in which property he was interested. From this place, which is about one hundred miles by the river above Bangor, thirty miles from the Houlton military road, and five miles beyond the last log-hut, I proposed to make excursions to Mount Ktaadn, the second highest mountain in New England, about thirty miles distant, and to some of the lakes of the Penobscot, either alone or with such company as I might pick up there. It is unusual to find a camp so far in the woods at that season, when lumbering operations have ceased, and I was glad to avail myself of the circumstance of a gang of men being employed there at that time in repairing the injuries caused by the great freshet in the spring.

The mountain may be approached more easily and directly on horseback and on foot from the northeast side, by the Aroostook road, and the Wassataquoik River; but in that case you see much less of the wilderness, none of the glorious river and lake scenery, and have no experience of the batteau and the boatman's life. I was fortunate also in the season of the year, for in the summer myriads of black flies, mosquitoes, and midges, or, as the Indians call them, "no-see-ems," make travelling in the woods almost impossible; but now their reign was nearly over.

Ktaadn, whose name is an Indian word signifying highest land, was first ascended by white men in 1804. It was visited by Professor J. W. Bailey of West Point in 1836; by Dr. Charles T. Jackson, the State Geologist, in 1837; and by two young men from Boston in 1845. All these have given accounts of their expeditions. Since I was there, two or three other parties have made the excursion, and told their stories.

Besides these, very few, even among backwoodsmen and hunters, have ever climbed it, and it will be a long time before the tide of fashionable travel sets that way. The mountainous region of the State of Maine stretches from near the White Mountains, northeasterly one hundred and sixty miles, to the head of the Aroostook River, and is about sixty miles wide. The wild or unsettled portion is far more extensive. So that some hours only of travel in this direction will carry the curious to the verge of a primitive forest, more interesting, perhaps, on all accounts, than they would reach by going a thousand miles westward.

The next forenoon, Tuesday, September 1st, I started with my companion in a buggy from Bangor for "upriver," expecting to be overtaken the next day night at Mattawamkeag Point, some sixty miles off, by two more Bangoreans, who had decided to join us in a trip to the mountain. We had each a knapsack or bag filled with such clothing and articles as were indispensable, and my companion carried his gun.

Within a dozen miles of Bangor we passed through the villages of Stillwater and Oldtown, built at the falls of the Penobscot; which furnish the principal power by which the Maine woods are converted into lumber. The mills are built directly over and across the river.

A Yankee in Canada
by Henry D. Thoreau

We left Concord at twenty minutes before eight in the morning, and were in Burlington about six at night, but too late to see the lake. We got our first fair view of the lake at dawn, just before reaching Plattsburgh, and saw blue ranges of mountains on either hand, in New York and in Vermont, the former especially grand. A few white schooners like gulls were seen in the distance, for it is not waste and solitary like a lake in Tartary, but it was such a view as leaves *not much to be said; indeed I have postponed Lake Champlain to another day.*

The oldest reference to these waters that I have met with is in the account of Cartier's discovery and exploration of the St. Lawrence in 1535. Samuel Champlain actually discovered and paddled up the lake in July 1609, eleven years before the settlement of Plymouth, accompanying a war party of the Canadian Indians against the Iroquois. He describes the islands in it as not inhabited although they are pleasant, on account of the continual wars of the Indians, in consequence of which they withdraw from the rivers and lakes into the depths of the land, that they may not be surprised.

"Continuing our course," says he "in this lake, on the western side, viewing the country, I saw on the eastern side very high mountains, where there was snow on the summit. I inquired of the savages if those places were inhabited. They replied that they were, and that they were Hiroquois, and that in those places there were beautiful valleys and plains fertile in corn, such as I have eaten in this country, with an infinity of other fruits." This is the earliest account of what is now Vermont.

The number of French Canadian gentlemen and ladies among the passengers, and the sound of the French language, advertised us by this time, that we were being whirled toward some foreign vortex. And now we have left Rousees Point, and entered the Sorel River, and passed the invisible barrier between the States and Canada.

The shores of the Sorel, Richelieu, or St. John's River, were flat and reedy, where I had expected something more rough and mountainous for a natural boundary between two nations. Yet I saw a difference at once, in the few huts, in the pirogues on the shore, and as it were, in the shore itself. This was an interesting scenery to me, and the very reeds or rushes in the shallow water, and the treetops in the swamps, have left a pleasing impression. We had still a distant view behind us of two or three blue mountains in Vermont and New York.

About nine o'clock in the forenoon we reached St. Johns, an old frontier post three hundred and six miles from Boston and twenty-four from Montreal. We now discovered that we were in a foreign country, in a station-house of another nation. This building was a barn-like structure looking as if it were the work of the villagers combined, like a log-house in a new settlement. My attention was caught by the double advertisements in French and English fastened to its posts, by the formality of the English, and the covert or open reference to their queen and the British lion.

No gentlemanly conductor appeared, none whom you would know to be the conductor by his dress and demeanor; but ere long we began to see here and there a solid, red-faced, burly-looking Englishman, a little pursy perhaps, who made us ashamed of ourselves and our thin and nervous countrymen.

BUSINESS LESSON

The traveler is to be reverenced as such. His profession is the best symbol of our life. Going from blank toward blank, it is the history of every one of us. There is nothing more refreshing than getting out of your "comfort zone" or "bubble" or "private prison." Travel as Henry did even if it's only within your immediate locale. Nature alone will revive you whether in your neighborhood or town square or backyard. Get out of the house . . . GET OUT! NOW!

Grab your favorite #2 and pencil in your business lesson here:

_____

_____

_____

17

TYING UP LOOSE ENDS

Any sincere thought is irresistible.

Loose End #1:
Calculating the Economics of Crime and Punishment

Source: Thomas J. Miceli, Economist

When Henry was still a young student at Harvard, he composed an essay on crime and punishment, according to University of Connecticut Professor of Economics Thomas J. Miceli in the 2020 summer issue of the *Thoreau Society Bulletin*. Henry wrote this essay, a requirement under the assigned theme "the comparative moral policy of severe and mild punishments," in September 1835 in the fall of his junior year. The coursework had directed all students to write biweekly "forensic" essays, argumentative papers on set themes, a condition of Harvard's academic stipulations.

Henry's essay specifically addressed the question of what the objective of punishment should be and what factors should come to bear on the determination of its severity. Miceli explains that "while this topic is of obvious intrinsic importance, the focus of my article is on how Thoreau's essay fits into the intellectual history of what has become a vibrant area of study at the intersection of economics and law, namely, the economic theory of crime and punishment."

Miceli continues: "The modern version of that theory had its origins in the seminal article, published in 1968, by the future Nobel Prize–winning economist Gary Becker. And while Becker's approach is fairly technical, making use of modern economic methods, he and subsequent scholars have acknowledged that the basic ideas underlying the theory—that criminal punishments can serve as implicit prices to influence behavior, and that they should therefore be chosen to channel that behavior in socially desirable directions—had clear precursors in the writings of three eighteenth-century philosophers: Charles Louis de Secondat (Montesquieu), Cesare Beccaria, and Jeremy Bentham."

The apparent gap between these early writings on crime and Becker's revival of this theme, however, has led some leading scholars in the field to observe that the subject of law enforcement has lain essentially dormant in economic scholarship for nearly two centuries. But lo! Miceli wants us to know that this is just not true! Henry, it turns out, as an *undergraduate college student* no less, developed ideas for his paper that bear a remarkable similarity both to the earlier writings and to the modern version of that theory. We'll let Professor Miceli pick it up again from here:

"Thoreau begins his short essay with the assertion that '*The end of all punishment is the welfare of the state,—the good of [the] community at large,—not the suffering of an individual.*' This reflects a clear utilitarian perspective on criminal punishment, which formed the basis for Jeremy Bentham's philosophy in general, and his approach to criminal law in particular. Bentham specifically argued that 'The general object which all laws have, or ought to have, in common, is to augment the total happiness of the community.'

"And Cesare Beccaria similarly observed 'The purpose of punishment . . . is nothing other than to dissuade the criminal from doing fresh harm to his compatriots and to keep other people from doing the same.'"

Miceli then observes that "modern scholarship on the economic theory of criminal law takes the same basic approach. As the article by Becker [cited above] describes it, 'The general problem of public law enforcement may be viewed as one of maximizing social welfare,' which [all these] authors define to be the aggregation of the benefits that people obtain from their (possibly illegal) actions, less the harm that those actions may cause and the costs of apprehending and punishing offenders."

A crucial assumption here is the perspective that at least some offenders act rationally and therefore can be deterred by the threat of punishment. Thus, as long as one crime is deemed more heinous than another, it becomes absolutely necessary that a corresponding distinction be made when punishing them. The earlier writers appear to have agreed:

"When two offenses are in competition, the punishment for the greater offense must be sufficient to induce a man to prefer the less," wrote Bentham, with Beccaria noting, "If an equal punishment is meted out to two crimes that offend society unequally, then men find no stronger obstacle standing in the way of committing the more serious crime if it holds a greater advantage." Montesquieu similarly asserted: "It is an essential point that there should be a certain proportion in punishments, because it is essential that a great crime should be avoided rather than a lesser one." All these views, Miceli comments, "reflect the deterrence motive for punishment."

Another key insight from an economic perspective on crime, Miceli adds, is that "complete deterrence is not the proper objective of a sensible policy . . . as there is an 'efficient' level of crime that is generally not equal to zero. [After all] preventing crime is a costly activity, and so resources should only be expended in this pursuit up to the point where the net gain from the last dollar spent is zero, i.e., to the point where the marginal benefit equals the marginal cost."

Miceli expands on this, introducing the more subtle point that "some crimes are inherently efficient because the gain to the offender exceeds the resulting harm to society." He cites the example of a driver speeding down the highway to the hospital in order to save an injured person. This idea of course would have made "perfect sense to Thoreau with respect to his own [belief] in civil disobedience. As he later would write, '*It costs me less in every sense to incur the penalty of disobedience to the State, than it would to obey.*'"

In keeping with this philosophy, Henry summarized his student essay, Miceli observes, with the following admonition: *We are not to act upon the principle that crime is to be prevented at any rate, cost what it may; this is obviously erroneous.* The fact that he found this assertion to be "obvious" may strike some as surprising, Miceli notes, yet it is a straightforward implication of an economic perspective on crime, and indeed is a foreshadowing of his own act of resistance later in his life.

All this raises the question of how Henry arrived at these views. Miceli suggests various potential sources that Henry might have come across but ultimately settles on what he feels to be the most likely explanation: that these ideas were simply "in the air" during Henry's time, an inference that can be drawn from Concord educator Franklin Sanborn's evaluation of Henry's essay: "Very noteworthy is his firm and concise grasp of the correct principle of Penalty."

As confirmation, Sanborn points to the work of Edward Livingston, one of the first to draft a criminal code in America. Published in 1833, this code was "designed to rationalize penal law on the utilitarian principle that Bentham had derived from Cesare Beccaria's famous treatise *On Crimes and Punishments . . .*"

Although deterrence is a familiar justification for criminal punishment in modern times, Miceli concludes, "It is inherently contradictory to the view, also commonly held, that criminals are somehow irrational actors. If the contrary idea that criminal behavior could be understood from a rational point of view was in fact pervasive during Thoreau's life, it seems to have fallen out of favor among criminologists by the mid-twentieth century. Indeed, the idea of a 'rational offender' had apparently become so unconventional by the time that Becker wrote his seminal article that he felt compelled to conclude with this following regrettable disclaimer: Unfortunately, such an approach has lost favor during the last hundred years . . . [Yet] by embracing that view, however he came by it, Henry therefore displayed a characteristically modern way of thinking."

That, and Henry's willingness to jump into the fray of calculating in hard cold cash economics a societal dilemma that for many reeks of rage, vengeance, and moral indignation, as opposed to a more coolheaded business approach *and potentially much fairer and more permanent wise solution.*

Loose End #2: Henry the Civil Engineer

Source: Henry Petroski, Thoreau Scholar/Author
Later in his life Henry Thoreau would at times have identified himself as a "civil engineer." While he would have had little inclination to join a professional society, given this was Henry, his story is relevant for an understanding of nineteenth-century engineering as well as for an appreciation of American transcendentalism. Thoreau's story, especially that of his involvement in the manufacture of pencils, has a lot in common with that of many nineteenth-century engineers.

First, many an engineer before mid-century, like Thoreau, would not have been certain that his activity was a profession at all, for one did not have to study engineering to practice it. College education prepared one for the ministry, law, medicine, or teaching; those who practiced and advanced engineering came to it largely through the crafts and the apprentice system.

Second, as in the case of Thoreau, innovative and creative engineering was done by those who were interested in a wide variety of subjects beyond the technical. Influential early nineteenth-century engineers could be a literate lot, mixing freely with the most prominent contemporary writers, artists, scientists, and politicians. And this interaction hardened rather than softened their ability to solve tough engineering problems.

Third, like Thoreau, innovative engineers tended to be iconoclastic and rebellious, rejecting traditions and rules. More than a few came from professional families that didn't understand why a young man would want to practice engineering. Those who succeeded as engineers stood out precisely because they could challenge the craft tradition for its own improvement.

Fourth, like Thoreau, most engineers practiced their trade without codifying it. There was little written by or about engineers before the middle decades of the nineteenth century, so there was little left for posterity telling the technical story of how and why certain designs or processes emerged. The theories of the pioneer engineers were tested by the erection of a solid bridge or the production of a good pencil.

Thus, major contributions to technology could be incontrovertibly demonstrated without a single word being spoken outside the workshop or committed to paper.

Proof of This Pudding: Many engineers, not all that surprisingly, are drawn to cooking and baking given the latitude of such a "hobby" to mix varying amounts of ingredients and experiment with new concoctions and recipes.

One day, in fact, Henry decided to have this same sort of fun while baking some bread, something he often did, so, looking around his kitchen, he grabbed at the first fun food he saw, tossing a handful of dried fruits into his mix, then adding hazelnuts. Once baked, he pulled it from the fire and sliced off a piece of his personal bread concoction, savoring the new flavor with approval.

Thus Henry's version of raisin bread was born, in this case spiked with hazelnuts!

Loose End #3: Henry Thoreau, Philosopher-Activist

Source: Henry's Journals

Do philosophers get paid? What about political activists? If paid for one's written ideas, even if philosophy and politics are embedded within a larger context or tangential theme, perhaps we could say that yes, they do. And we could then say that Henry has been foremost among them in America's history given the abundance of thoughts he had written out and writ large and expressed sincerely. As he once wrote:

> *To be a philosopher is not merely to have subtle thoughts, nor even to found a school, but so to love wisdom as to live according to its dictates, a life of simplicity, independence, magnanimity, and trust.*

So when one considers all of Henry's essays, poems, journals, books, and letters, Henry certainly lived the part of the above quotation. Review these samplings of such *"wisdom according to life's dictates"* he expressed over the course of his lifetime:

A Plea for Captain Brown (lecture, book published posthumously)

You who pretend to care for Christ crucified, consider what you are about to do to him who offered himself to be the savior of four millions of men . . . I am here to plead his cause with you. I plead not for his life, but for his character—his immortal life; and so it becomes your cause wholly, and is not his in the least. Some eighteen hundred years ago Christ was crucified; this morning, perchance, Captain Brown was hung. These are the two ends of a chain which is not without its links. He is not Old Brown any longer; he is an angel of light.

On Civil Disobedience (essay, book published posthumously)

I heartily accept the motto "That government is best which governs least"; and I should like to see it acted up to more rapidly and systematically. Carried out, it finally amounts to this, which also I believe— "That government is best which governs not at all"; and when men are prepared for it, that will be the kind of government which they will have. Government is at best but an expedient; but most governments are usually, and all governments are sometimes, inexpedient.

The objections which have been brought against a standing army, and they are many and weighty, and deserve to prevail, may also at last be brought against a standing government. The standing army is only an arm of the standing government.

The government itself, which is only the mode which the people have chosen to execute their will, is equally liable to be abused and perverted before the people can act through it. Witness the present Mexican war, the work of comparatively a few individuals using the standing government as their tool; for, in the outset, the people would not have consented to this measure.

Walking (journal, lecture, essay, book published posthumously)

When we walk, we naturally go to the fields and woods: what would become of us, if we walked only in a garden or a mall? Even some sects of philosophers have felt the necessity of importing the woods to themselves, since they did not go to the woods. "They planted groves and walks of sycamores."... Of course it is of no use to direct our steps to the woods, if they do not carry us thither.

I am alarmed when it happens that I have walked a mile into the woods bodily, without getting there in spirit. In my afternoon walk I would fain forget all my morning occupations and my obligations to society. But it sometimes happens that I cannot easily shake off the village. The thought of some work will run in my head and I am not where my body is,—I am out of my senses. In my walks I would fain return to my senses. What business have I in the woods, if I am thinking of something out of the woods?

Henry's Influence on Social Reform

The consequence of this kind of outpouring of thinking and passion has been, throughout history since Henry's time to today, a significant influence from those who came after him. As a social reformer and political thinker, whose lingering thoughts have especially spotlighted one's duty to resist injustice no matter its source, Henry's thinking has guided the likes of Mohandas Gandhi, Martin Luther King Jr., Leo Tolstoy, John Muir, Emma Goldman, and many others. Virtually every country in the world has been touched by his clarion

call to embrace human rights over political rights, derived specifically from his essay *On Civil Disobedience*.

My good friend and comrade-activist Ron personally handed me
a copy of this essay during the height of the Vietnam War. I read it
thoroughly (pun intended!) and found it powerful enough to mobilize
me into the anti-war movement and take action to do whatever I
could to end what seemed to be an obviously inhuman enterprise.
Before being made aware of Henry's declaration of independence, I
had only vaguely heard of Henry and yet now he was cornering me
exactly where I lived.

> *Can there not be a government in which the majorities do not
> virtually decide right and wrong, but conscience? Must the
> citizen ever for a moment, or in the least degree, resign his
> conscience to the legislator? Why has every man a conscience,
> then?*

With a polemic such as this, Henry could surely have developed
a specialized "branding" drawn from incidents like the one night
he spent in Concord's jail for refusing to pay his poll tax, due to his
disgust with the Mexican War, or for his activism in the abolition-
ist movement, specifically as a major player in the underground
railroad, or for his rage at the bloodshed at Harper's Ferry. These
deep dives into right/wrong also affirm and reinforce how Henry
approached business matters, revving up with the same passion to
deliver superior customer satisfaction via hard work, smart work,
going-the-extra-mile work, and, not least, ethics!

Loose End #4: Simply God

As a philosopher and transcendentalist, Henry clutched tightly to
his values here as well, seeking God by peering with a pantheistic
sense into simple spirit, in the process shunning bias in favor of one
religious modal above all others.

I do not prefer one religion or philosophy to another. I have no sympathy with the bigotry and ignorance which make transient and partial and puerile distinctions between one man's faith or form of faith & another's . . . To the philosopher all sects, all nations, are alike. I like Brahma, Hari, Buddha, the Great Spirit, as well as God.

Thus, it seems clear that even in such ever-shifting human factors as trust, outrage, tolerance, and action items, Henry's business instincts carried him in the proper direction of every moment of every day.

BUSINESS LESSON

Live in each season as it passes; breathe the air, drink the drink, taste the fruit, and resign yourself to the influence of the earth. There is so much we can all do our lives if we only get out and give things a try. See the varied expanse of Henry's efforts in so many different disciplines and areas of potential interest. Let's find out what exciting new things can happen to *you!*

Grab your favorite #2 and pencil in your business lesson here:

_____

_____

_____

18

EPILOGUE

He is the rich man, and enjoys the fruits of riches,
whose summer and winter forever can find delight
in his own thoughts.

In the last year of Henry's life, as he weakened and was overcome by the growing scourge of tuberculosis, the real hero of his life emerged. The fatal disease had taken so much of what he loved away from him: leaving him too weak to go off on four-hour or even four-minute explorations of Walden Woods, too weak to scout for arrowheads in the dirt around Egg Rock or record the comings and goings of new flowers sprouting along the trail at Walden Pond, too weak to play the flute for the neighborhood children or the ice workers at Ice Fort Cove.

Perhaps worst of all, Henry was now too powerless to even think about conceiving a new poem or, god forbid, beginning a *third* book! Though Waldo would have come by now and then sit with him a short while, and likely Bronson Alcott too, and even his good friend from Worcester, Harrison Gray Otis Blake, such visits had to stretch fewer and further between as Henry's condition worsened.

Henry's only surviving sibling, Sophia, recognized this and took it upon herself to nurse him while he struggled with daily persistent coughs, fatigue, and fevers. Sophia could see that not much was left to do except ensure that his life waned as comfortably as possible, which meant, in specific, coaxing him out of bed each morning, then setting him down in the Thoreau living room. Their big yellow house on Main Street in Concord was so quiet now with only their mother still left, but even so Henry could bear being up and about for not much more than a few hours.

One morning as Sophia was upstairs dusting Henry's attic apartment where he used to sleep and write, she found his many unfinished essays, letters, attempts at new poems, and other writings. Perhaps struck by a sudden epiphany that morning, Sophia challenged herself to do *more* than just dust and play nursemaid. Or perhaps Henry himself said it outright to Sophia one day, in almost a whisper: "Sophia, I would like to finish my work before I go. Would you help me with that?" But in any case, Sophia decided she would do more than just prop Henry up on the living room couch to gaze mournfully out the window for hours each day.

The good news is that Sophia was probably better suited than the rest of his family or friends—even his lifelong mentor, Waldo—to help Henry resume his writing. Sophia and Henry shared some personality traits such as a potential for sudden mood swings and the capacity to explode when confronted with injustice or a cutting remark—and the incapacity to ignore it. But more important, they shared a commitment to creativity. Sophia too was literary-minded, although she was less of a writer and more of a five-star editor and document organizer, a role she handled expertly after taking the reins of Thoreau Pencils so Henry could write. Sophia was also a talented artist. Her depiction of Henry's cabin still adorns the title page of *Walden*—Henry could have chosen another artist's work but decided that Sophia's captured it best.

So we might imagine that one morning, after settling Henry onto the couch, Sophia left the room, returning minutes later with a tall stack of his papers. "Let's see what we've got here," she must have said, followed by each of them carefully picking out one item after another, reading each item through, discussing whether anything next needed to be done, then noting their decision and moving on to the next item. Likely their purpose was *not* for Henry to attempt to write anything more but to merely define whether a finished essay might be ready for publication, either in a magazine or in book form such as *Walking* and *Cape Cod* would one day become. Such outcomes might take many years to transpire, but Sophia would take whatever steps were needed.

The work went on for as long as Henry could maintain his strength and attention, until finally, too weak to continue, he began staying in bed day and night as if only waiting for the final moments to arrive. This became so trying as time went on that, on what would be his very last day, he could utter only one word here and there. In his last hours, he managed to push out *moose* and *Indian*, but no more. That is, until, in a last gasp of expression, Henry formed a full sentence as if suddenly lit up with a burst of understanding that his time had come to move things along. "Now comes good sailing," he remarked clearly and simply. His end was nigh.

Not long after that, presumably on his way to a final excursion, Henry passed. Not a resting place exactly, but rather, as he had articulated, another business venture. As a sailor, and likely *captain* of his ship, he would next be in command of a vessel that would help him, like Darwin and his HMS *Beagle*, seek out and discover newer worlds. This was the opposite of what we term dying. For Henry, this would instead mark a life "renewed," as he had wished for his time in the tiny house he had built mere footsteps from Walden Pond.

Sophia Takes the Baton

Following his demise, Sophia picked up the pieces of all that was still left to be done with Henry's writings and legacy. She became his postmortem literary agent, taking the baton from Waldo, Horace Greeley, Bronson Alcott, Nathaniel Hawthorne, and so many of Henry's other good friends and advocates. Now with the mission squarely in Sophia's able hands, this final phase, she knew, would be strictly business.

As was true with whatever her brother set out to do, Sophia met the challenge, achieving publication for many of Henry's final essays in multiple editions of *The Atlantic Monthly* as well as in book form mainly via Boston's Houghton Mifflin. Then—lo and glory hallelujah!—in 1895, a full volume of Henry's poems, *Poems of Nature*, would be published not only by Houghton but in London too by UK publisher John Lane. Henry had finally made the grade, not just as a writer of prose but as the sort of writer he had dreamed about in his youth: a professional, acclaimed, world-famous poet!

Sophia also persuaded the Concord Free Public Library to accept Henry's papers for storage and perpetual availability to scholars. The result is that Henry continues to live with us today, reviewed and analyzed by scores of authors of new books every year. Plus, *Walden*—his masterpiece—continues to sell robustly to this day, cherished by thousands (if not millions) of readers who credit him with shaping their worldview and guiding principled, practical business decisions.

Letting go of Henry was hard for his friends, family, and the world, as he gave so much. But when we assess him solely through a business lens, he shows us how to integrate our businesses and careers with qualities often confined to personal life: empathy, ethics, creativity, reflection, social justice, good cheer. We might imagine him now, still "good sailing," gliding from one natural paradise to the next, skimming atop another wondrous kettle pond like Walden, not far from his latest hand-built cabin. This time the waters truly *are* bottomless and no barriers divide business success from personal fulfillment.

HENRY FACTS

In addition to Sophia's drawing of Henry's cabin at Walden Pond, she also left a unique memorial to her brother in the form of five shagbark hickory tree leaves bearing twenty-eight lines of what is considered by some to be his final published poem, titled "Fair Haven," reproduced here in its entirety:

When little hills like lambs did skip,
And Joshua ruled in heaven,
Unmindful rolled Musketaquid,
Nor budged an inch Fair Haven.

When principle is like to yield,
To selfish fear, or craven,
And fickle mortals round me fall,
I'll not forget Fair Haven.

If there's a cliff in this wide world,
'S, a stepping stone to heaven,
A pleasant, craggy, short hand cut,
It sure must be Fair Haven.

Oft have I climbed thy craggy steep,
Where ceaseless wheels the raven,
And whiled away an hour at e'en,
For love of thee, Fair Haven.

If e'er my bark be tempest-tossed,
And every hope the wave in,
And this frail hulk shall spring a leak,
I'll steer for thee, Fair Haven.

When cares press heavy on my soul,
And devils blue are craven,
Or e'er I lay me down to rest,
I'll think of thee, Fair Haven.

And when I take my last long rest,
And quiet sleep my grave in,
What kindlier covering for my breast,
Than thy warm turf Fair Haven.

AFTERWORD

In addition to the spectacular legacy that Henry has left us with regard to his published essays and journals and books, especially *Walden*, one further example he seems to have left us with was his capacity to separate business affairs from transcendentalist principles. Astonishingly, perhaps the most remarkable example of this legacy presented itself many years after his death . . . 128 years to be exact!

As the story goes, the legendary recording artist Don Henley, a cofounder of the Eagles, had flipped on the CNN at his home in Los Angeles in 1989 when a report aired featuring two Thoreau scholars, Tom Blanding and Ed Schofield, who were leading an effort to stop the development of two major commercial projects virtually next door to Walden Woods, including Walden Pond.

It seemed that one property developer had proposed constructing a 147,000-square-foot office building on Brister's Hill, a nearby lot in the very heart of many natural surroundings that Henry himself had traversed multiple times. In fact, Henry had studied Brister's Hill extensively on a personal quest that would eventually establish a groundbreaking scientific theory on forest succession, a precursor to modern ecological science, deeming Henry, to many, the "father" of the environmental movement.

Not far from Brister's Hill, a second property developer had proposed a 139-unit condominium complex to be "planted" atop a gorgeous, forested area in Walden Woods called Bear Garden Hill, one of Henry's favorite "sauntering" destinations and the inspiration for many of his essays and journal entries.

As an admirer of Henry since the mid-1960s, Henley grew increasingly concerned as the news report went into details. To Henley, a commitment he must make seemed obvious: to not only oppose these projects that would undermine the historic and environmental integrity of the treasured Walden Woods but to establish a non-profit organization as well, ultimately under the name of the Walden Woods Project, that could raise funds to buy the endangered sites from the two developers and to further the preservation of other historic sections of the 2,680-acre Walden Woods.

The late author E. L. Doctorow, referenced by Henley in an article published in *Discover Concord* magazine, once said it this way:

> We need both Waldens, the book and the place. We are not all spirit any more than we are all clay; we are both and so we need both: You've read the book, now see the place. You have to be able to take the children there and to say, "This is it—this is the wood old Henry wrote about. Do you see?" You give them what is rightfully theirs, just as you give them Gettysburg because it is theirs.

That fateful day when Henley switched on CNN and soon chose to join the fight to save Walden Woods and Walden Pond from commercial development led to explosive support for the Walden Woods Project from people in countless walks of life—writers, political leaders, environmental and historic preservation activists, dozens of people from the entertainment industry, and numerous citizens from across the United States, all participating in their own ways to preserve Walden Woods as a national treasure via letter-writing campaigns, walk-a-thons, petitions, articles, fundraising concerts, and so forth, all aimed at protecting the land and legacy of Henry David Thoreau.

The result has meant the permanent protection of the two sites once endangered by commercial development that now safely thrive under the stewardship of the Walden Woods Project, where the public engages in peaceful recreation and benefits as well from educational offerings, particularly customized for school groups. The Brister's Hill site, for example, incorporates and honors the dual legacy of Henry and the formerly enslaved Brister Freeman, for whom Brister's Hill is named. Freeman also fought in the Revolutionary War.

So despite Henry's innate business acumen, he firmly believed that commerce and profit should never be allowed to plow through woods, fields, wetlands, birds' nests, indigenous flowers, and so on, nor trade off Henry's name or sacred spaces.

Might Henry's very spirit have been guiding the trajectory of the efforts of Henley and so many other Thoreauvians? Only the essence of business genius Henry can say for sure . . .

APPENDIX

Henry Builds His Cabin
Builder, bean-field farmer, careful accounting + P&L, research, social good, ethics, goal-setting, risk/sacrifice

Henry Invents the Pencil
Pencil engineer/inventor . . . struggle, rejection, problem-solving, research, imagination

Henry the Master Surveyor
Surveyor . . . careful accounting + P&L, details & observation, sauntering, networking, chatting, research, social good, ethics, goal-setting, risk/sacrifice, courage

Henry the Writer
Struggle, rejection, problem-solving, details & observation, sauntering, networking, chatting, research, auditions, tryouts, practice, social good, ethics, imagination, goal-setting, courage

Henry's Innovative Teaching Methods
Research, social good, ethics, imagination, risk/sacrifice, courage

Henry the Public Speaker
Research, auditions, tryouts, practice, social good, ethics, imagination, goal-setting, risk/sacrifice, courage

Henry's Scientific Bent
Details & observation, sauntering, networking, chatting, research

Henry the Civil Engineer

An inquisitive inventive mind who appreciated how things were constructed and how they might be improved or even reinvented

Henry Lands in Jail

Social good, ethics, risk/sacrifice, struggle, courage, as citizen activist, underground railroad, John Brown, tax resister

Philosopher Henry

Details & observation, sauntering, networking, chatting, auditions, tryouts, practice, imagination, risk/sacrifice, courage

Henry the Handyman

Attention to details & observation, imagination

Henry's Marketing Savvy

Entrepreneur/manager/decision-maker/executive/marketing expert . . . bean-field farmer, careful accounting + P&L, details & observation, imagination, risk/sacrifice, courage

Master Henry, Tutor

Struggle, rejection, problem-solving, sauntering, networking, chatting, research, social good, ethics, imagination

Henry Explores Many Lands

Details & observation, sauntering, networking, chatting, research, risk/sacrifice, courage, travel writing

CHRONOLOGY OF HENRY'S LIFE EVENTS

NOTE: This life chronology is based on the version assembled by Jeffrey S. Cramer for his book *The Portable Thoreau*. I've made a few adjustments to align with contents in *Walden for Hire*.

1817 born David Henry Thoreau, July 12, third of four children—Helen (1812–1849), John (1815–1842), and Sophia (1819–1876)—to John and Cynthia (Dunbar) Thoreau in Concord, Massachusetts.

1818 Family moves to Chelmsford, Massachusetts, where father opens a grocery store.

1821 Grocery store closes; family moves to Boston where father works as a schoolteacher.

1822 Visits Walden Pond for the first time.

1823 Family moves back to Concord, where father begins making pencils; family takes in boarders.

1828 Enrolls in Concord Academy, as does his brother, John, where they study geography, history, and science as well as French, Latin, and Greek.

1829 Attends lectures at the Concord Lyceum.

1833 Enrolls in Harvard College.

1835 To earn money, teaches in Canton, Massachusetts, during winter term.

1836 Leaves Harvard temporarily due to illness.

1837 Graduates from Harvard; starts journal; friendship with Emerson begins.

1838 Travels to Maine for the first time to search for a teaching position; gives first lecture, "Society," at Concord Lyceum; elected secretary and curator of the Lyceum; opens small private school before taking over the Concord Academy in September.

1839 John joins Thoreau at Concord Academy as a teacher; Thoreau meets Ellen Sewall, to whom both he and John will propose and by whom both will be rejected; takes boat trip with John on the Concord and Merrimack Rivers to Concord, New Hampshire.

1840 *The Dial* first published, for which Thoreau will be a contributor and sometime editor; teaches himself surveying.

1841 Concord Academy closes due to John's poor health.

1842 John cuts himself while stropping his razor and dies of lock-jaw, January 11; Thoreau meets Nathaniel Hawthorne; climbs Mount Wachusett; publishes "Natural History of Massachusetts" in *The Dial.*

1843 Tutors William Emerson's children on Staten Island, New York; publishes "Paradise (to Be) Regained" in *The United States Magazine and Democratic Review.*

1844 Accidentally burns three hundred acres of woodland, causing more than $2,000 in damage; helps build the family's "Texas House" in southwest Concord; reinvents the pencil.

1845 Builds and moves into a small house at Walden Pond, July 4; begins writing *A Week on the Concord and Merrimack Rivers.*

1846 Begins writing *Walden*; spends night in jail for nonpayment of poll tax; climbs Katahdin in Maine.

1847 Gives lecture "A History of Myself," an early draft of *Walden*, at Concord Lyceum; leaves Walden Pond on September 7, moving in with Emerson family while Emerson is in Europe; collects specimens for Louis Agassiz at Harvard.

1848 Publishes "Katahdin" in *Sartains Union Magazine*; gives lecture "The Relation of the Individual to the State" ("Civil Disobedience").

1849 Publishes *A Week on the Concord and Merrimack Rivers*; publishes "Resistance to Civil Government" ("Civil Disobedience") in Elizabeth Peabody's *Aesthetic Papers*; sister Helen dies of tuberculosis; travels to Cape Cod for the first time.

1850 Family moves to house on Main Street, Concord, where Thoreau will live for the remainder of his life; goes to Fire Island, New York, at Emerson's request, to search for the remains and papers of Margaret Fuller, who died in a shipwreck; travels to Canada.

1852 Publishes excerpts from *Walden* in *Sartains Union Magazine.*

1853 Publishes parts of *A Yankee in Canada* in *Putnam's Monthly*; travels to Maine for what will be the basis for "Chesuncook."

1854 Publishes "Slavery in Massachusetts" in *National Anti-Slavery Standard, The Liberator*, and the *New York Tribune*; publishes *Walden; or, Life in the Woods*; lectures in Philadelphia.

1855 Grows throat beard, also known as Galway whiskers, early in the year; publishes parts of *Cape Cod* in *Putnam's Monthly*; receives gift of forty-four volumes of Asian literature from Thomas Cholmondeley.

1856 Surveys in Perth Amboy, New Jersey; meets Walt Whitman in Brooklyn.

1857 Meets John Brown; grows full beard; makes final trip to Maine.

1858 Publishes "Chesuncook" in *The Atlantic Monthly*; travels through the White Mountains and climbs Mount Washington, July 2–19.

1859 Father dies; becomes financially responsible for family; delivers his first public support of John Brown in "A Plea for Captain John Brown."

1860 Reads Charles Darwin's *On the Origin of Species*; catches cold that turns into bronchitis, precipitating his tuberculosis.

1861 Visits Minnesota for his health in May, returning unimproved in July; visits Walden Pond for the last time in September; begins revising his writings for posthumous publication.

1862 Dies May 6 of tuberculosis; buried May 9 in New Burying Ground, Concord, and later reinterred on Authors Ridge at Sleepy Hollow Cemetery.

CHRONOLOGY OF HENRY'S WRITINGS

1827 Thoreau wrote student essay "The Seasons," his earliest known composition.

1837 Thoreau began to keep a journal.

First published piece, obituary notice of Anna Jones, appeared in Concord newspaper *Yeoman's Gazette*.

1840 Published pieces in *The Dial* (poem "Sympathy"; essay "Aulus Persius Flaccus").

1841 Published poetry in *The Dial* ("Stanzas," "Sic Vita," "Friendship").

1842 Published essay ("Natural History of Massachusetts") and poems (including "To the Maiden in the East") in *The Dial*.

1843 Published in *Boston Miscellany* ("A Walk to Wachusett"), in *The United States Magazine and Democratic Review* (essay and book review), and in *The Dial* (poems, including "Smoke"; essays, including "A Winter Walk"; and selections in translation from Oriental literature and from Chaucer).

1844 Published lecture extracts ("Homer, Ossian, Chaucer"), essay ("Herald of Freedom"), and translations in *The Dial*.

1845 Published letter ("Wendell Phillips Before the Concord Lyceum") in *The Liberator.*

1847 Published "Thomas Carlyle and His Works" in *Graham's Magazine*.

1848 Published "Ktaadn and the Maine Woods" in *The Union Magazine*.

1849 *A Week on the Concord and Merrimack Rivers* appeared (Boston: James Munroe and Company).

Published "Resistance to Civil Government" in Elizabeth Palmer Peabody's *Aesthetic Papers*.

1852 Published what would later be parts of *Walden* in *Sartain's Union Magazine*.

1853 Published "Excursions to Canada" in *Putnam's Monthly Magazine*.

1854 Published in *New York Daily Tribune* (selections from soon-to-be-published *Walden*) and in *The Liberator* ("Slavery in Massachusetts").

Walden; or, Life in the Woods appeared (Boston: Ticknor and Fields).

1855 Published "Cape Cod" in *Putnam's Monthly Magazine*.

1858 Published "Chesuncook" in *The Atlantic Monthly*.

1860 Published in *The Liberator* ("The Last Days of John Brown") and in *New York Daily Tribune* ("The Succession of Forest Trees").

1862 "Walking," "Autumnal Tints," and "Wild Apples" published posthumously in *The Atlantic Monthly*.

1863 Previously unpublished pieces appeared in *The Commonwealth* and *The Atlantic Monthly* ("Life Without Principle" and "Night and Moonlight," both in *Atlantic*).

Excursions (edited by Sophia Thoreau and Emerson) appeared (Boston: Ticknor and Fields).

1864 Journal extracts published in *The Commonwealth*, "The Wellfleet Oysterman" and "The Highland Light" in *The Atlantic Monthly*.

The Maine Woods (edited by Sophia Thoreau and Ellery Channing) appeared (Boston: Ticknor and Fields).

1865 *Cape Cod* (edited by Sophia Thoreau and Channing) appeared (Boston: Ticknor and Fields).

Letters to Various Persons (edited by Emerson) appeared (Boston: Ticknor and Fields).

1866 *A Yankee in Canada, with Anti-Slavery and Reform Papers* (edited by Sophia Thoreau and Channing) appeared (Boston: Ticknor and Fields).

1878 Extracts from journals published in *The Atlantic Monthly.*

1881 *Early Spring in Massachusetts* (edited from journals by H. G. O. Blake) appeared (Boston: Houghton Mifflin).

1884 *Summer* (edited by Blake from journals) appeared (Boston: Houghton Mifflin).

1888 *Winter* (edited by Blake from journals) appeared (Boston: Houghton Mifflin).

1892 *Autumn* (edited by Blake from journals) appeared (Boston: Houghton Mifflin).

1894 *Familiar Letters of Henry David Thoreau* (edited by F. B. Sanborn) published (Cambridge: Riverside Press).

1894 Riverside Edition of collected writings (eleven volumes, including the four volumes from the journals as edited by Blake) published (Boston: Houghton Mifflin).

1895 *Poems of Nature* (edited by Sanborn) published (London: John Lane; Boston and New York: Houghton Mifflin).

1905 Journal extracts appeared in *The Atlantic Monthly.*

1906 *Walden* and manuscript editions of collected writings (twenty volumes, including the fourteen-volume *Journal*) published (Boston: Houghton Mifflin).

1971 First volume of "Princeton Edition" of collected writings published (publication ongoing to date).

1972 *Thoreau's World: Miniatures from His Journal* (Prentice Hall).

1993 *Faith in a Seed* (Island Press).

1999 *Wild Fruits* (W. W. Norton & Company).

FINAL THOUGHTS FROM HENRY'S FRIENDS

Q&A WITH LAWRENCE BUELL,
TRANSCENDENTALIST SCHOLAR/AUTHOR/SPEAKER

What would you say if someone asked you what Henry did "for a living"?
Henry was a classic example of "living on lack of expense" so he could pursue the kinds of living that meant more to him.

How would you characterize Henry's attitude toward "work"?
Hostile in principle to the conventional work ethic, nevertheless "internalized" dutifulness in laboring for another and observed a scrupulous worth ethic on surveying projects that mattered to him or in his own primary pursuits, which he pursued *ferociously.*

Do you wish Henry had spent more time in one endeavor or another? In other words, if you had been his "career coach," what might you have advised him to do more of, to stick with, to give up, etc.?
His poetry was a false start. He might have enjoyed school teaching more if he'd stuck with it—but then again the world might have been deprived of a misfit's wonderful genius. I would not have wanted to be his career coach. Emerson tried and got his fingers burned. Horace Greeley also tried, and Thoreau disregarded Greeley's advice to compromise for the mass market.

Q&A WITH RICHARD SMITH, AUTHOR/SPEAKER/HISTORICAL INTERPRETER

What was Henry able to do well in a work-related area and/or accomplish that you envy?

He was very single-minded at whatever he was doing. His powers of concentration were phenomenal! I actually think that he would be diagnosed with OCD today. I wish I could be that concentrated when I'm writing (or doing any kind of work, for that matter).

What were Henry's weakness(s) when it came to work/career/ business?

I think the single-mindedness was also a curse at times. He drove editors crazy! If he wrote something, he was very adamant about it not being changed in any way. When James Russell Lowell edited one of Thoreau's essays without consulting him, Thoreau refused to send any more submissions to *The Atlantic Monthly* so long as Lowell was editor. He did the same thing when George William Curtis cut a couple of lines that Thoreau sent to *Putnam's Magazine*.

What should people know about Henry in relation to work/career/ business that they do not know today?

That writing was not his main occupation, that he did other things to earn money. Most people don't know that he was a surveyor.

What would most surprise people today about Henry's work/ career/business life that is not in the popular image of his life and persona?

That when he wrote his books and essays that he expected to be paid for his work. People think that he was anti-money, or that he didn't care if his books sold or not. Not true! We have several letters from him to various publishers and editors asking when is going to get paid for his submissions.

You don't become a writer and hope that your books don't sell! I think that Thoreau would have been very happy had he become a financially successful writer.

CHUCK HANSEN, AUTHOR OF *BUILD YOUR CASTLES IN THE AIR: THOREAU'S INSPIRING ADVICE FOR SUCCESS IN BUSINESS (AND LIFE) IN THE 21ST CENTURY*

What was Henry able to do well in a work-related area and/or accomplish that you envy?
I wish I were as productive and prolific. Thoreau not only thought the thoughts and walked the walk (literally!) but he also put pen to paper and gifted the world with his remarkable prose. An hour spent wandering through the product of Thoreau's mind can yield a lifetime of enrichment. We are lucky he was so dedicated to this work.

What should people know about Henry in relation to work/career/ business that they do not know today?
In his masterpiece, *Walden,* and in many of his other works, Thoreau brings a stunning clarity of thought and insight into an increasingly grinding twenty-first-century work experience. His wisdom is not only for the rank and file, who are most often on the receiving end of "stretch goals," but also for their managers, many of whom are trying to find a humane way to manage their employees while simultaneously carrying out the often-inhuman demands of business.

What would you say if someone asked you what Henry did "for a living"?
What Henry David Thoreau did "for a living" was what every successful businessperson does: He thought deeply, reflected honestly, and assessed situations with a clear eye. Then he took the results of this work and put them out into the world, and his "product" reflects that work.

All too often at work we rush to and fro among self-ignited fires, never stopping to consider to what better purposes we could be dedicating our flint and sparks. Forget day to day, quarter over quarter, even year over year—Thoreau's business cycle could be counted across millennia, and his focus and priorities were calibrated accordingly.

Q&A WITH LAURA DASSOW WALLS,
AUTHOR OF *HENRY DAVID THOREAU: A LIFE*

What would you say if someone asked you what Henry did "for a living"?
First I'd point to his passage in *Walden* about the true cost of a thing being the amount of life we are willing to exchange for it—which means that he'd smile at the very phrase "what you do for a living," and say something like, "You must get your living by loving." (As of course he does say in "Life Without Principle"! [RP 160]) So, "what you do "for a living" is *not* "make a lot of money" doing something you hate, in order to do what you really want to do somewhere else, in some other part of your life.

So I'd say that while he tried to radically redefine our relationship to work, meaning that what we do for "work" should be something that we do for love rather than money, he also had the practical problem of earning money. So he chose work that was meaningful and either contributed to a larger cause, such as teaching (in which he innovated in exciting and creative ways) and pencil-making (a craft occupation, producing a fine and useful product for all, from schoolchildren to carpenters, artists, and engineers), to land surveying (which did give him some qualms, but which he largely enjoyed doing)—or else, something that he could do that was needful and useful for someone else, as in manual labor, which he did willingly and well.

How would you characterize Henry's attitude toward "work"?
Henry thought it was a tragic mistake to divide work from life, labor from love—and so he tried to redefine work as a creative, purposeful contribution to one's own life, but also to the life of the community.

What work and/or business lessons did Henry develop or adopt?
He was proud of the high quality of the pencils he and his father developed and made, and after his father died, his eulogy honored his father's attitude toward work: which was, to treat making pencils (and their other products as well) as a form of art. His father, said Thoreau, brought artistry to the making of even common objects, and grace to the act of service to others. Henry learned from this. Take his surveying: The finished surveys are beautiful objects, completed with skill and elegance. And in the process of surveying, when he was in the act of performing a service for his clients, he tried to create at the very least a courteous social relationship; clearly the best jobs were those during which he could use the surveying process as a means to teach his clients something about their land, and learn something from them about local history: a relationship of mutual exchange. Whenever a client refused this courtesy, Thoreau got grumpy and angry in his journal, impatient and short-tempered. He clearly loathed being reduced, while at work, to a "tool" for someone else.

Do you wish Henry had spent more time in one endeavor or another? In other words, if you had been his "career coach," what might you have advised him to do more of, to stick with, to give up, etc.?
Well, I think the cranberry venture was doomed from the start. But hey, he learned something even from the failure! In fact, I think this is true of his other less-than-successful "career" attempts: Editing *The Dial* with Emerson was a frustrating time-suck, but he learned from it, both about precision in editing and that editing was not the best use of his skill set. He learned from the failed tutoring job on Staten Island that he wasn't good at working with dull students.

The one thing I wish he'd done, as a writer learning the work of writing, was to listen more closely to Horace Greeley's advice to start out by writing more short pieces for publication, before spending years on the long first book. Refusing Greeley's wise advice closed the door on Thoreau's nascent career in commercial writing. But again, he learned from that failure too—he always turned failure into reinvention, and grew each time. And frankly, he wouldn't have listened to anyone who offered "career coaching" anyway! After all, Emerson tried that, and it nearly ruined their friendship.

What was Henry able to do well in a work-related area and/or accomplish that you envy?
Easy: his technical expertise, his ability to work out a problem with an engineer's mind, figuring out how machines work, how to invent them, fix them, critique them. He was totally unintimidated by machinery, factories, technological systems: They didn't scare him at all. He dove in and talked with the engineers, the workers, the managers, anyone, eager to understand everything he could. I envy that—Henry wouldn't pass by the huge faceless new Amazon warehouse and grumble. He'd go inside, watch, ask questions, observe . . . and then he'd incorporate what he learned into his next essay. Imagine what he'd have written about Amazon! He'd have gone to the heart of all the problems, laid out the errors in reasoning (including ethical errors, on their part and on ours), and insisted on the need to make radical changes.

What was/were Henry's weakness(es) when it came to work/career/business?
He was terrible with the paperwork. Thank goodness his sister Sophia was so good at it. She pretty much took over that side of the family business after their father died.

What should people know about Henry in relation to work/career/ business that they do not know today?

Henry was the absolute opposite of lazy: Whatever work he turned to, he did full tilt, and to the highest standards. The common assumption that he slouched around, bummed off his friends and family, couldn't be bothered to do a day's honest work—to know his biography is to find that infuriating. He was the kind of guy you turned to whenever you needed something—pretty much anything—done. He'd figure out how to do it, and do it, and do it well.

The best example, and the one that still amazes people who still don't know it, is that Henry invented the common pencil and the machinery to make it. And that the Thoreau family became prosperous because of Henry's work in the family business.

Anything to add?

I've seen so many promising young people graduate, get the big glitzy job that pays a lot of money, then write me years later that they're miserable and they wish they had listened to me back when we were studying Thoreau together. It's tragic. It takes remarkable courage to follow a path like Thoreau's, but I hope more young people today find that moral courage within themselves, because otherwise we will all have a much more miserable future. Thoreau dreamed of pursuing a path, "however solitary and narrow and crooked, in which I could walk with love and reverence." I wish that dream for my students, and I hope some of them find that path.

I'm still paging through "Life Without Principle": *A man had better starve at once than lose his innocence in the process of getting his bread.*

ACKNOWLEDGMENTS

First and foremost executive editor of HarperCollins Leadership Tim Burgard not only immediately saw the value of this book but moved quickly to make a commitment to me to get it published and to support every step of the process from then on. Tim has proven to be a smart, insightful editor and a burgeoning new friend. Thank you, Tim!

Thanks as well to expert resources who have helped me out along the way, including Director Anke Voss and her team at the Concord Free Library special collections section; copyeditor Mikayla Butchart; Beth Kessler and Jeff Farr at Neuwirth & Associates, Inc.; the amazing team at Faceout Studio for the cover design and Ron Huizinga for the art direction; Kate Kelly of WETA for help with PBS; and the following Thoreau scholar-authors who have given of their time to me in a Q&A Zoom session as well as their published works: Laura Dassow Walls, Larry Buell, Jeff Cramer, Chuck Hansen, Richard Smith, Corinne Smith, Mike Frederick, Tom Miceli, and Patrick Chura.

In addition, other contributors whose published articles, essays, and commentary benefited this book include Walden Woods Project Executive Director Kathi Woods and Assistant Director Juliet Trofi for their great help with the book's afterword, as well as George Comeau, Richard Primack, Patrick Garner, Oshan Jarow, John Roman, and Mark Whittaker. Thank you all!

Special shout-out to Elena Petricone, my DIO (deputy imaginative officer) at emerson consulting group, inc., a skilled novelist, short story author, and editor in her own rite, who not only encouraged me excitedly from day one but kept the emersongroup fires burning (and contained!) during days and weeks when I turned my attention to this book exclusively. Elena, I cannot express nearly enough how valuable you have always been to me, and continue to be.

To my immediate family: Ed & Ginny Lizotte, Rob Litwak & Liz Liptak, Nick Henriquez, I thank you for your unwavering and ongoing support which has meant the world to me.

As well, to my daughter, Chloe Elizabeth, a brilliant, published writer many times over, and gifted editor and professional film critic, you have always been in my corner and excited both for me and this book. You are the very best of the very best, in all things, a bright shining star.

Finally, of course, a million thank-yous to my lifelong faithful companion, Barb, for your patient and continual support despite my lengthy "fortress of solitude" disappearances as I researched, outlined, scribbled notes, wrote, rewrote, edited, tweaked, and so on, off and on, for five years! I adore you now and forever.

INDEX

ABOUT THE AUTHOR

The author seated at a replica of
Henry David Thoreau's writing desk.

KEN LIZOTTE CMC, CEO of emerson consulting group, inc., has transformed over 450 business experts, professional service firms, private companies, and nonprofit organizations into "recognized thoughtleaders" since founding his firm in 1996. By helping his client thoughtleaders spread their ideas via books, articles, speaking engagements, and media presence, he empowers them to separate themselves and their firms from the "competitive pack."

The author of eight previous books, Ken has also been a regular columnist for *HuffPost, Money Inc.*, the American Management Association, and *Boston Magazine*.

A veteran public speaker, Ken's speaking credits include hundreds of keynotes, breakouts, and panels at national and regional events throughout the United States as well as virtually. A cofounder of the National Writers Union, graduate of Alan Weiss's Million Dollar Consulting College, and an active national board member and chapter president of the Institute of Management Consulting, he resides in Concord, Massachusetts, with his family, a short three-mile run to Walden Pond and back again.

To learn more, visit www.thoughtleading.com.

THOREAU FARM,
THE BIRTHPLACE OF HENRY DAVID THOREAU

Ken also serves as pro bono president emeritus of the Board of Trustees at Thoreau Farm, the birthplace of Henry David Thoreau, guiding the publication of two popular volumes of volunteer Thoreau essayists tasked with their personal answers to the question posted by the titles.

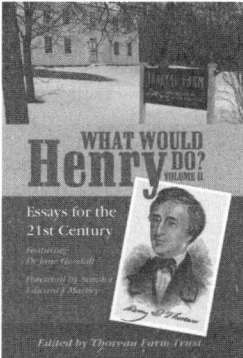

What Would Henry Do? Essays for the 21st Century, Volume II, featuring a Q&A with Dr. Jane Goodall with a foreword by US Senator Ed Markey (2022)

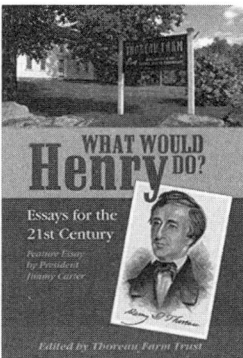

What Would Henry Do? Essays for the 21st Century, Volume I, featuring lead essay by President Jimmy Carter (2017)

Thoreau Farm Trust is a nonprofit organization committed to preserving Henry's birth house and birth room, promoting his extraordinary insights into life, nature, and social responsibility. To achieve its mission, Thoreau Farm sponsors educational programs that present Henry's birthplace and surrounding landscape as a source of inspiration for living deliberately, practicing simplicity, and exploring new ideas for positive change.

To learn more visit www.thoreaufarm.org.